What About the Church?

Other Books by the Stendals

1. *Rescue the Captors I*. The personal testimony of almost five months in the hands of Colombian guerrillas.

2. *Rescue the Captors II*. A new book - a new adventure. This book picks up where *Rescue the Captors I* leaves off.

3. *The Beatitudes - God's Plan for Battle*. Learn to walk according to the ways of God and overcome the enemy.

4. *The Jubilee Bible*. The Jubilee Bible is much more consistent translating the same thing the same way (within the limits of the English language).

5. *Spanish Books*. Russell has written a number of Spanish titles under the name *Martin Stendal*.

Books by Chad Stendal

1. *The Guerrillas Have Taken Our Son*. Chad and Patricia Stendal share their side of Russell's kidnapping.

2. *High Adventure in Colombia*. Testimony.

3. *This Gospel of the Kingdom*. The true gospel that will be proclaimed in all the earth before the end shall come.

What About
the
Church?

What God demands from his people in the end times

Russell M. Stendal

LIFE SENTENCE
Publishing, LLC

www.lifesentencepublishing.com

Like us on Facebook

What About the Church? – Russell M. Stendal

Copyright © 2013

Scripture taken from the Jubilee Bible®. Copyright © 2000 by LIFE SENTENCE Publishing. Used by permission. All rights reserved.

PRINTED IN THE UNITED STATES OF AMERICA

First edition published 2013

LIFE SENTENCE Publishing books are available at discounted prices for ministries and other outreach. Find out more by contacting info@lifesentencepubishing.com

LIFE SENTENCE Publishing and its logo are trademarks of

LIFE SENTENCE Publishing, LLC
P.O. BOX 652
Abbotsford, WI 54405

Paperback ISBN: 978-1-62245-092-3

10 9 8 7 6 5 4 3 2 1

This book is available from www.lifesentencepublishing.com,

www.amazon.com, Barnes & Noble, and your local Christian Bookstore

Cover Designer: Amber Burger

Editors: Sheila Wilkinson & Ruth Zetek

Share this book on Facebook

Contents

These 6 booklets have been compiled in this single volume,
What About the Church?

A Different Kingdom
Message 53

THE PLAN OF GOD FOR HIS FRIENDS

RUSSELL STENDAL

The Plan of God for His Friends

A message on sharing God's love with others

Russell Stendal

LIFE SENTENCE
Publishing, LLC

The Plan of God for His Friends

--·--===≈===--·--

The following was given at a meeting in Bogota about ten years ago. I was going to preach on John Chapter 17 and at the last minute a very high ranking Guerrilla leader walked into the auditorium and sat down! So my message changed to: God's Plan for His Friends.

Every time this place fills up I think we will need a bigger place to hold the meetings. Then the Lord takes some of the people to another place, and we get some of our space back so that we can fill it again. And who would have thought that the messages that leave this place have been heard all over Colombia and Latin America via the radio and people, who have distributed them on cassette and compact disk. This can only happen if there is a concerted effort made by all. This is different from preaching alone before a microphone in a cold sound studio.

When the majority of the audience members are good Christians, people with clean hearts, the Lord can bless us with good messages. Our intention here is not to tie anyone down; we are not trying to form another sect or denomination; we are not trying to control people's lives in manipulating them by means of their tithes. We only want you to walk circumspect before God and man.

I don't even think that going to church is an indispensable part of the Christian life, because there have been large portions of history when Christians were not able to congregate. Up until five hundred years ago, we didn't even have printed Bibles; and the majority of the common people didn't know how to read.

Today, most of the things that seem central to religion don't have much in common with the true religion that our Lord taught us. Our Lord taught that real religion is to accompany the widow and the orphan in their afflictions and not let ourselves be tainted by the world (James 1:27).

This means we may have to endure hardships because we will accompany widows and orphans and share what we have with them, to the point that we also feel the hardships that they are experiencing. Why? Because we are helping them to the point that we also start to feel the pinch. This is contrary to greed and avarice. If a small portion of the people, especially the leaders of Colombia's privileged class, understood what the Bible says about true religion, there would not be so many poor people in need.

To not be contaminated by the world means that we don't do things the way the world does them. The world is full of corruption and if one negotiates, has a place of importance, or does anything in this world, unjust and unseemly things will happen. So, real religion in the words of our Lord does not even mention paying tithes, going to church, crying, or screaming. It doesn't even mention reading the Bible.

True religion, according to the Lord, pertains to a different behavior in the measure of how the heart has been changed. I dare say that the people who read the Bible and go to religious services with their hearts full of corruption, not only find that these things avail them nothing, but could also find that these things put them in a worse condition than if they did nothing. Corruption in the spiritual realm is the worst form of corruption, because the people who say they represent God are in fact doing the opposite.

We know that corruption has permeated our society in economic and political areas, but the corruption that exists in the religious part of our society is more serious and disastrous, because religious people are the ones who are forming the next generation. If these people are teaching things in the name of God and are not clean (even if they are teaching good things), they transmit more of their attitude and corruption than the message that comes out of their mouths. One generation then passes this on to the next, generation after generation.

The same thing can happen to children in schools. They are taught a subject called religion, but most of them don't even pay attention to what they are being taught if they see that the teacher is a liar and full of greed. So they learn to behave as their teacher behaves, or they reject everything the teacher says. Consequently, either more religious people are formed who are even worse hypocrites, or more rebellious people are formed who don't want to know anything about God. Good men and women cannot be formed unless there is a cleansing.

A good friend of mine was a sled dog champion in Canada. Some races lasted for as long as eight days in extreme freezing temperatures. Imagine a sled dog race that was fifteen hundred kilometers long. The participants in this sport learned that in order to compete they must have hybrid dogs, so they started mixing up the breeds. Then they learned that to have an extra edge they had to mix in some wolf blood, so they did. The only problem is that wolves by nature are very wild and are not the same as domestic dogs. So in a bad situation, some people found out that they could be attacked and maybe even killed by their own sled dogs.

When I visited my friend, his dogs always seemed tame, even though they were also crossed with wolves, so I really didn't trust them. One day I asked him, "Why do you have such tame dogs, when others have savage dogs that will even kill their owner?"

He answered me, "Very simple. When a puppy first opens its eyes, what it sees is imprinted onto its personality and spirit. If its mother is a savage wolf, the puppy grows up to become the same by instinct and nature. To avoid this, when the puppies first open their eyes, I take them into the house and have them play with my children, so what is imprinted on my sled dogs is my children. These puppies are tame all their lives and have a different personality than other wild dogs."

His dogs won the races because they put their whole hearts into pleasing their owner. This was clearly seen in his lead dog (the one that motivated the other dogs) who, when he was old, had a permanent leaning of his head to one side, and his ears pulled back to the same side, because he had spent all his life leaning his head and pulling his ears to that side in order to hear his master's voice behind him. These dogs, instead of being controlled by harnesses and reins, were controlled only by their master's voice commands. The master would issue a command, and they would obey whatever it was.

I remember the time I was in Canada, and it was minus thirty degrees. My friend had his fifteen dogs hitched to the sled, and the sled was tied to a water pipe that was staked into the ground and served as a brake. A Colombian friend who was with me had never been in Canada before, so I passed him the camera and told him to get in front of the sled to take our picture when the sled took off.

Who would have imagined what was going to happen next! The traditional Inuit word for the dogs to start racing is *mush*. Imagine a race where everyone has a whole bunch of sled dogs programmed for this word, and someone carelessly says *mush*. So my Canadian friend had decided to program his dogs to start on the word *okay* instead.

My friend did all right and took three pictures and then said, "Okay, Russ, I took the pictures." Those dogs took off like lightning, bending the three-quarter-inch galvanized water pipe they were tied to like it was butter. They caught my Canadian friend off guard and threw him from the sled into the snow. I was left alone on this sled, not knowing how to control the dogs.

My friend saved the day when he screamed at the top of his lungs for the dogs to veer to one side, and since he was in an agitated state, the dogs obeyed immediately, turning over the sled in the process. I ended up under the sled with one of my boots caught, being dragged around in the snow until I could unhook my boot. Even after my friend had caught up with the dogs and managed to control them, I still had to run as fast as I could to throw myself onto the sled.

This was the experience of a lifetime, but can you imagine God's problem with us when we won't obey His commands? And to make matters worse, His commands are voluntary. The people who obey God's commands are those who want to walk in His ways; they are the ones who don't want to be free to go their own ways, even though those ways might seem better at times.

Mistakes are not easily pardoned in the freezing temperatures of North America. One mistake can take you far out of your way when you are out with a team of sled dogs. The mistake may seem small, but it can have serious consequences. Just letting your glove fall to the ground could cause your hand to freeze, and you could lose some of your fingers because of the intense cold.

I don't know if we knew enough or if we just had enough faith in God (probably both), but I realized that I could hold conferences all over Canada and Alaska – and the conferences would be well attended – because few people wanted to go to those freezing locations. We realized that the best time for us to visit was in the winter, and we were always well received.

Also, we had lots of friends all over these places. When our meetings were announced, people would show up from all over and from all denominations, without caring what day of the week it was. It's not like here in a city of millions where we are lucky if we get a hundred people to show up.

In addition, these people help each other on the road. If someone has car trouble or there is any kind of a situation, nobody drives by without stopping and asking if you need help, because in those temperatures you could die. I didn't know that it is not customary for people to go out when it goes below minus forty degrees. After minus fifty degrees, the oil in your car even starts to freeze. If one continues in these conditions, the possibility of ending up stranded is very high, and you can't last long.

They had told me that only true friends would visit in the winter because there is hardly any sunlight due to the earth's rotation. In summer there is lots of light. I have been there when the sun never sets; it just goes around in the sky but doesn't go down. In winter, it does the opposite; during that part of the year, the sun never rises. You can drive north until you get to where there are only four to five hours of daylight; you barely see the sun, and then it disappears.

So we went up to where there is no pavement, and after many miles, the road turns into a frozen river (where the ice is a couple yards deep), and then you come to the ocean. We then drove on the ocean until we finally came to the last Inuit village named Tuktoyaktuk, which has a population of about three hundred. We got there and didn't know why we hadn't seen anyone else driving on the road, not recognizing the danger we had been in. We learned that the natives only leave their houses if it is a matter of life or death.

An interesting thing we realized is that we had better visibility when we were in total darkness than when we had twilight. This is because the darkness contrasts against the lights of the vehicle, whereas the partial twilight makes the vehicle lights blend in with the twilight to the point of not being able to distinguish between the two.

This is a good lesson: When things are all mixed up, it is more difficult to orient ourselves. It is preferable for things to be very dark or very light so that we have better discernment. But wait till I tell you what happened on my return trip. We left at midnight under a rush as there was a storm brewing. I wanted to get out of there before the blizzard obstructed all passages, and we got stuck. As we left, we passed by the last gas station, which was closed, but since I had driven up there on one tank of gas and I carried two full five-gallon containers with me, I thought it would be enough. But something happened.

When we came out of the blizzard, everything became light, and we drove until dawn started to break into a clear, bright day with no clouds. I said, "Well, we got through the worst. Now we are safe. We left the bad part behind."

But what I didn't count on was that as long as we were in the storm, the cloud cover maintained a temperature that didn't go below minus thirty or thirty-five degrees. Without the cloud cover, the earth loses its heat faster, and the temperature can drop to dangerous levels.

I soon noticed that it was minus sixty-seven degrees. When this happened, the car started consuming double the gasoline. When I realized this, I was almost out of gas. We had the car's heater on full blast and hadn't recognized what was happening outside. But praise God, we were able to get to the nearest gas station, safe and sound. In those extreme freezing temperatures, a person is not able to walk even one kilometer without freezing to death. It was so cold that while I was in the restaurant next to the filling station, the hydraulic oil in the power steering froze, and steering the car became difficult for a while.

Through all of this, I realized that there are times when people think that they are all right, but in reality they are not. In this world's system, which is full of corruption, there is no hope for a true peace. Instead, the world only produces a false peace, causing many to think they are at peace when they really aren't. I think this is the case for most major cities in the world.

Many people walk the streets up and down and think everything is all right. They think things are getting better, when in reality these people are in grave danger. Why are they in danger? Because sooner or later they will have to give an account for what they are and what they have done. This could happen suddenly, and it will be a surprise to many people.

After filling my car with gas, I continued on my way and ran into a friend who thought no one was going to come see him that winter. I got to his house, and his wood floor was so cold it was steaming. We sat in the dining room on top of the table with our feet up on the chairs because the floor was too cold.

Later, when I set out to visit other friends, I remembered I had to return a cassette to someone who had loaned it to me. I put my hand into my bag to get it, but I cut my finger on the razor blade in my bag. When I got there, they had to bandage my hand. Everything was going so good that I said, "God has his hand in this." I asked the Lord why I had to put my hand in my bag and get cut like that.

I felt in my spirit the answer, "Because you are not careful. Not only that, but you are walking around in some very dangerous situations as if it were nothing." So the next time, I made sure to top off the gas tank every time I saw that it was three-quarters full.

I continued my trip and stopped at a hotel because the fog was too thick to drive in. So obeying the voice of the Spirit, I got a hotel room. Everybody had their cars parked there, all with their electrical heaters plugged in, and the motors running. You also need to have synthetic oil and lots of antifreeze in the radiator. I tried shutting off the vehicle and plugging it into the electricity and went and took a bath.

Two hours later, the car would hardly start. I was hesitant to leave it running all night as I had heard you shouldn't do that, but everyone was doing it. So after starting it and turning it off about three times, I started it again, left it running and went to sleep. When I woke up, someone was shouting, "Fire!"

I went out to see, and it was my car that was on fire. In that cold temperature, the air is denser and fire burns better and faster. We couldn't put it out. We almost burned down the hotel and everything else. And instead of a car, all we had left were charred remains.

My brother had loaned me this car under many protestations, saying it was the best car he had ever owned. It belonged to my brother and my dad, and it had been difficult to persuade both of them to let me borrow it. Now that it was destroyed, we ended up having to tow it with another car to get it away from the building, and then it exploded twice. I don't know how we weren't all killed.

When they evacuated the hotel, there were all these ladies in their nightgowns out in the minus sixty-seven-degree weather, looking for the one responsible for their inconvenience, and I was the one responsible. The fire truck came, but it was too late, and it didn't do much good anyway as they were having trouble because the water was freezing almost before it could get from the hose to the car.

The most interesting part of that trip was that my message (and I thought it was a beauty) was titled, "The Fire of God." It's very easy to preach a good message to everybody, but it is not so easy living the message. The message is not ours, and the Lord will not bless us until we have made the message a part of us, a reality in our own lives. If we are preaching one thing and doing another, we cannot count on the blessing of God. Sadly, this is the case in many places; the message that is preached is not lived.

Well, I had to call and tell my brother and my father what happened to their car. They told me to report it to the insurance company. The car was insured with a company located close to Miami, Florida, where there is never this kind of cold. I had to explain to the insurance lady twice where I was in Tok, Alaska.

After a while, she called me back and asked me where the other car on the insurance policy was, and I said, "In the garage."

She said, "And where is the garage?"

I said, "The garage is in Bonita Springs, Florida, at my brother's house on the Gulf Coast of Florida."

She said, "That's good. I was afraid you were going to tell me it was in Africa or something."

The curious thing is that the people in the next hotel room were heading to the same place I was, so they took care of me and got me where I needed to be. When it came time to leave, the insurance company took me at my word, and even though the car was in my brother's name, they issued the check in my name. I got on a plane and came back to Colombia with the insurance check in my pocket.

My brother was in Puerto Lleras, Meta (Colombia) asking me to meet with Wycliffe Bible Translators. They were selling everything at Lomalinda (in late January of 1996) and leaving the country, and this was our opportunity to buy their farm and some houses. I got there and gave them the check as a down payment on three houses. This is now where we have several radio stations. But in a thousand years, I never would have thought to buy those houses, if I hadn't had that check in my pocket.

Those houses remained unlived in for several years. They were ransacked and vandalized in the midst of the civil war, and we had no idea why we had them. That is, until one day, I got a phone call from a church in Florida, and they said, "We feel you should have a radio station there in Colombia." They said it could be a big contribution towards peace in the region where we work. They continued by telling me, "We have this offering we would like to give you to be used towards your radio station."

It was about two thousand dollars, and I thought, "How are we going to get a radio station for two thousand dollars? Somebody should tell those people that radio stations are very expensive." But since our policy has always been to honor a giver's request, we set aside the money and didn't touch it, waiting to see how we were going to use it for a radio station. Several times I almost called them to see if I could use it for something more urgent, but instead, I left it alone, waiting to see what would happen.

About this time, our long-time friend and fellow missionary Ray Rising was released after being kidnapped. He had been Wycliffe's radio man at Lomalinda, and he was in agreement with the radio station idea. So, he sent me to some places in Florida where they sell radio equipment. I got there and told them what I needed, and they got me the basics: a transmitter, some antennas, some coax cable, and some other things. They told me, "It costs eight thousand dollars, but since it's for a good cause and you are nonprofit, our policy is to give a fifty percent discount."

I sadly told them that when I had the money I would be back. Then the manager whom I had never met before said, "Wait, wait. How much do you have?" When I told him I only had a little over two thousand dollars, he said. "Our company can't give you any more discounts, but I like you, and I feel in my heart that I should help you out, so I will pay the difference out of my personal account."

With those words, I was dispatched, and when I returned to Colombia, no one bothered me coming through customs, even though I had all the radio equipment in my suitcases. I had an old stereo and some friends had a recorder. I put all this equipment in my car and headed out to the Llanos (southeastern plains).

When we got to Bonaire (my brother's farm), we didn't have a tower, we didn't have all the stuff we needed, but we did have a flagpole. So I got someone to climb up the flagpole and attach the antenna at the top so we could try out the equipment. We were doing this when a teacher from the town of Puerto Lleras showed up on a bicycle and asked me what we were doing. I said we were just trying out some stuff.

He said, "Looks like a radio transmitter."

I said, "Yeah, yeah."

He asked, "Do you have a license?"

I said, "No sir, I don't have a license. I am only trying out my equipment to see if it got here undamaged."

So then he floored me with the following words, "I have the license." He left and started calling his friends.

As it turned out, there had been a scandal in the Pastrana government in the Ministry of Communications, and most of the new radio station licenses were revoked, and they wouldn't issue them anymore. They had only issued about five or six licenses, one of those being the one given to the Communal Cultural Association, managed by the teachers of Puerto Lleras, Meta. These teachers were in a pinch because the Ministry of Communications had given them a certain time limit to put their station on the air, and they didn't have any equipment, in spite of having been able to extend the time limit for an extra year.

I got there just in time for them when I started trying out my equipment on the flagpole. So we made a deal, and Marfil Estereo on

88.8 FM was born. As time went on, we acquired more equipment and even a powerful signal that could be heard all over the area.

Our relations and the trust with this group of teachers have broadened with time, despite our different opinions. In all of this, I have found that our differences are not so important as to cause division among us. Any one person or a particular group can be radical in their way of thinking. Ideologically, they can believe that their position is one of superiority, but what defines the situation for me is the attitude of the heart.

When people are not interested in furthering a personal agenda, real success can occur. What do we gain if someone can talk eloquently, but behind that eloquence, they are only seeking personal gain? I prefer to work with someone who, even if I believe them to be wrong in their thinking, shows a sincerity of heart. If I see that they are not taking advantage of the circumstances for personal benefit and are willing to serve others, even if they are faulty in their thinking, I would prefer to work with them. It is preferable to have cobwebs in the head instead of the heart.

I know religious people who seem to have a clear head and have everything in order in their lives. They teach in Bible schools or theological seminaries or elsewhere. The only problem is that some of these people seem to have many cobwebs in their hearts. If the heart is in bad condition, the remedy is much harder. If we are really seeking the truth, we are seeking a cleansing of our hearts.

I have had to change many of my doctrines and personal ideas down through the years and in varying circumstances. I remember times with Zacarías (my recently-renewed friend) years ago when we would sit in Mapiripán and argue politics. Today, we don't even think about those times, and we can hardly even remember what our differences were.

Now I am not concerned if he has a different opinion from mine, nor is he worried about that either. Why? Because we have forged such a close friendship from the heart to the point that I have no problem putting my life in his hands, nor does he in putting his life in mine. We can trust each other with our eyes shut. That is what God is looking for in each of us. People are looking for the truth, but they don't know that our Lord is named *Truth*.

I was invited to debate the president of the Atheist Association. We met in a friend's office, and many were gathered for this event in what became an atmosphere like before a cock-fight, with each person betting on his rooster to win. They brought me in for the fight, and I was innocent. I had no idea what was going down when they brought in this doctor of atheism, a brother of some high politician. The atheist started out saying, "I am the very antithesis of everything Russ stands for. See what Russ is, and you will see I am everything contrary to what he is."

So started the debate: Is there a God or isn't there? I said, "Well, doctor, before we begin, I would like to ask you a question. Do you love the truth? Would you be willing to die for the truth?"

He said, "Of course, I would."

I said, "Are you sure?"

He said, "My whole life has been devoted to the truth, which is what I am all about."

So I answered, "Well, doctor, I want to tell you something. You are not my enemy because I serve the Lord Jesus, and He is the Truth in person. If you love the Truth, then you love Him. There is a misunderstanding of terminology, but we are potentially on the same side. We are colleagues."

The debate ended right there. Afterwards, the atheist told the friend who had set up the debate, "Invite me again sometime. I would like to talk more with Russ."

Many times, the fights start over something totally unnecessary, but behind it all, I believe what keeps the fight going is not ideology or doctrine, but rather the corruption in human hearts. Corrupt people are pulling for their own side and trying to blame circumstances, other things, or people, and it turns into a vicious circle that only gets worse.

I have been out walking in the jungles, rivers, and towns and have learned some things. First, I made it a point to travel around with lots of people because I thought if we ran into trouble the enemy would respect us more if there were more of us. It is nice to take people with me so they can see things for themselves. However, lately I have been in some circumstances where the orders have been, "Don't touch Russ, but kill whoever is with him, and that will stop what he is doing."

So, I got the idea to travel alone, because if I am alone, they won't kill anyone. I have made about five trips this way to some very turbulent zones where I would never have been able to visit any other way. When I meet anyone, no matter what group they're from, they can't believe that I would be out there alone, and when they see that I am, they tend to respect me more. Not only that, but they feel they can open up and tell me things from the heart because they respect me.

On the other hand, if I take another two or three people with me, and the people don't know who they are, they won't really open up and tell me what is in their hearts. So going alone is one way to break the ice. It is also the best way.

A few years ago when I started dating my wife, Marina, a pilot friend gave me some very bad advice that almost got me killed. He said, "Look Russ, if you want to save six months of work dating her, to break the ice, all you have to do is put her in the airplane and get into a dangerous situation. When it starts to get very turbulent and the bottom starts to drop out from under her, she will get all scared and grab you, thus avoiding months of work to get to this point."

But when I tried this with Marina, it didn't happen like that. I sat her in the airplane, and we headed to Mapiripán. Big clouds loomed over Casibare, so instead of going around them, I remembered what my friend had said and took the plane right into the storm. When it started lightening right in front of our noses, and the plane shook in the extreme turbulence, she didn't hug me; she went completely crazy. She wanted to get out of there and started fighting me for control of the airplane. When I wouldn't let her have it, she attacked me physically. I ended up losing in that fight, and I felt like going to find my friend and strangling him for his bum advice that almost got us both killed.

All this is to say the following: There is a way to do things and a way NOT to do things, and only the Lord can show us the way, how to do it and when to do it. By the grace of God, we have been in many tough circumstances and here we are still. The Lord has given us the wisdom not only to survive the circumstances, but also to get through them and make many friends in the process.

At this time, many of the rural areas of Colombia are not in good shape. It is difficult to see who is winning this war, but I know who is definitely losing and that is the poor campesino people in the rural areas. There is a need to extend real friendship to whoever is willing to join us. Where there are people who are clean in the armed forces, who are not seeking their own ends, they should join with us in friendship.

How can we find a solution with a group of people sitting around a table when they are a bunch of hypocrites with grave blemishes on their hearts, and where they say one thing and do another? We can never find a solution that way. For this conflict to be resolved, we must find people with integrity, who are transparent, not seeking their own agenda, and willing to risk their lives for the good of all. These are the people who can truly contribute to a lasting peace.

When I was interviewed by Todelar (a national radio chain), I was asked if I thought Colombia really wanted peace. I told them that it was too broad of a question, but that I thought many Colombians do want peace. I also told them with certainty that any person who participates in corruption is against peace, in spite of what he may say. In my opinion, whatever is said by corrupt persons has no validity.

First, we must heal the problem of corruption, and only afterwards can we talk about peace. It would seem we have a formula: The one we are implementing now is about to destroy the world for everyone. But the Lord wants to change that, and He wants to get us all out of this mess.

We are not so ignorant as to believe that we can sit down with everyone and achieve a real peace. Peace will be achieved person by person, heart by heart, and this is the peace plan that we are trying to implement. It's reaching people one by one wherever we can find them. A person's decision to walk in uprightness with a clean heart must begin in their own home and among their circle of friends.

You may find ten policemen in a station where only one or two of them are clean. The remaining eight must decide to either shape up and start working in the same manner as the two clean ones or get rid of them if they want to continue in their corruption. The clean ones don't have to be the majority. Even with ten percent clean people, you can still have a big effect.

We speak of this group or the other. We speak of the army or the police. Many times we speak of things that certain individuals do within these groups. If at some time people in a certain group no longer seek their own ends, turn toward the truth, and become employed in serving others to the point of risking their own lives, a great difference will be obvious when comparing them to others within the same group who don't have this same attitude. We have seen it many times.

You can even find this same difference between one church and another. I had the opportunity to visit many Catholic churches with the late Padre García Herreros. I saw Catholic churches that are in much better spiritual condition than some evangelical churches that I know. Why? Because of corruption.

I would rather work with a Catholic priest who has a clean heart than an evangelical pastor whose heart is full of problems and greed. What is better? The better thing (according to the Scriptures), if we want good fruit and a good effect, is that we must have clean hearts and clean minds. But if we can only have one of the two, I prefer the ones with clean hearts, even if they have faulty doctrine and crazy ideas. This is the decision I have made. I have found that people with clean hearts will always be good friends and will always be thinking of others before themselves.

Do you remember the parable Jesus told of an old man who had two sons? The first son said to his father, "Yes father, I will go do your work," except that he never went and did it.

The other son apparently was more rebellious and said, "No father, I will not go and do your work," but later he did go and do the work of his father.

And so the Lord asked the question, "Which of these two sons did the will of the father? Was it the one who promised but didn't go, or the one who refused and did go?"

Today there are many people who don't know much about God. Earlier I spoke about the president of the Atheist Association who attempted to debate me. As it turned out, some people had come to his home, and in the name of God they had done much damage to him and his family. He had reacted by going to the opposite extreme. But even then, he said he was seeking the truth and was willing to die for the truth. These are the kind of people we need. What purpose can we have with people who merely say, "Yes, I believe in God, I believe in the Bible, I believe all the right doctrine," and yet live from one lie to the next?

And here we begin our Bible study in John 17, which is the prayer Jesus prayed to His Father, the prayer that He made as High Priest to mediate the new covenant with us. By this, I mean that He came, did what He had to do, and went back to His Father with the purpose of implementing this covenant with us. He has the power and the authority to do it. The only thing lacking is our agreement.

> 1 *Jesus spoke these words and lifted up his eyes to heaven and said, Father, the hour is come; clarify thy Son, that thy Son may also clarify thee,*

The problem we have here on earth is that those who say they are God's people are not operating in a way that *clarifies* God. It is not clear who God is to them. The world thinks that God is a tyrant, a monster, and everything contrary to who He really is. Or else the world thinks God is a softy who winks at everything wrong they do.

> 2 *as thou hast given him power over all flesh, that he should give eternal life to as many as thou hast given him.*

If we are going to come to the Lord, the Scripture says that the Father must draw us. And the Father sees the hearts of all people and knows whom He is going to draw and whom He isn't going to draw. He knows who loves the truth. He knows who loves integrity. I have seen people out in the jungle whose hearts are in a better state – even while participating in what looks like open rebellion – than other people who go to church every Sunday.

3 And this is life eternal, that they might know thee the only
true God and Jesus Christ, whom thou hast sent.

Note that He doesn't say that eternal life is our life that goes on forever. Eternal life is another quality of life, and it is a quality of life that we cannot know without knowing the truth in the person of God who is the only truth.

4 I have clarified thee on the earth; I have finished the work
which thou didst give me to do.

5 And now, O Father, clarify thou me with thine own self
with that clarity which I had with thee before the world was.

The Lord is not in agreement with this world because the world does things according to the prince of this world. John 8:44 says that Satan, the prince of this world, is a murderer and a liar from the beginning. So, the Lord wants us to know the clarity that was before all this, when everything was good.

6 I have manifested thy name unto the men which thou didst
give me out of the world; thine they were, and thou didst give
them me; and they have kept thy word.

The men God gave to the Lord Jesus were not religious and did not run the systems of this world. They were fishermen. They were not rebellious. They were the ones He chose, the ones He picked up from around there. But of Nathanael, He says in John 1:47, *Behold a true Israelite, in whom is no guile!* The ones He chose were not hypocrites, and that is what He was looking for.

7 Now they have known that all things whatsoever thou hast
given me are of thee.

8 For I have given unto them the words which thou gavest
me; and they have received them and have known surely

that I came out from thee, and they have believed that thou didst send me.

9 I pray for them; I do not pray for the world, but for those whom thou hast given me; for they are thine.

The ones who truly belong to the Lord, wherever they are found, love integrity and are not hypocrites. Terminology is not the most important thing to the Lord. Even ideology is not as important as the heart. If there is sincerity in the heart, sincerity to seek the truth, the Lord accepts that person. In the churches, they talk so much about accepting the Lord, and I know we can accept the Lord, but don't you think it is more important that the Lord accept us?

One day in Canada, I was working on a book that was later published here. I am not sure if it was *Rescue Your Family* or if it was the last portion of another book. But I was in the mountains of Canada. Lisa, my daughter, was small, and she had the habit of jumping down the stairs two at a time. Why? Because she clung to my hand. As I held her hand, she could do whatever she wanted and not get hurt, because I had a secure hold on her.

One day we were walking, and I didn't realize I didn't have a good grip on her; she was only holding onto my finger with her little hand. So when we came to some stairs, she just jumped without thinking about it. She didn't have enough strength in her hand to hold onto me, so she went tumbling head over heels with me after her. I thought she was going to break her neck because she tumbled over and over, down two flights of stairs, and she fell on her head. But I couldn't do anything about it. Fortunately, everything turned out all right.

But we can experience similar situations with disastrous results if it is only us clinging to God. But if God is holding onto us, it is going to be all right. We can seek God, and we can give ourselves to God.

I am not saying we should not do these things, but we can't have the same confidence if we are doing these things by ourselves.

Instead, if it is God drawing us, if God is seeking us, if God accepts us, if God is holding onto us, then we are truly secure in His grip. And He is seeking something. He doesn't choose just anyone. He says he can't stand hypocrisy; He can't stand those who are seeking a lie. He wants people of integrity who are seeking the truth wherever they are. When God invites people to the feast, if there are some among them who name the name of God but don't come, then He will invite those who will come, those that are His out of all walks of life. He can call them wherever they are and use them.

> 8 *For I have given unto them the words which thou gavest me; and they have received them and have known surely that I came out from thee, and they have believed that thou didst send me.*

> 9 *I pray for them; I do not pray for the world...*

The Lord is not praying that all be well with those who are corrupt in the world, with those who are doing terrible things. He is praying for those who want the truth.

> 9 *...but for those whom thou hast given me; for they are thine.*

> 10 *And all my things are thine, and thine are mine; and I have been clarified in them.*

The person who truly belongs to the Lord will share what he has wherever the Lord shows him to do so. This is the reason that we don't ask for tithes and offerings; we are asking that people give themselves totally to the Lord and do what He tells them to do and to give their time and resources wherever the Lord wants them to.

The Lord never asked people for their money. He did tell the rich young ruler in Luke 18:22 to *sell all that thou hast ... and follow me.* And He said, *distribute [it] unto the poor.* This is unlike many of today's preachers who tell people they must give what they have to the church or to the pastor or preacher himself. The Lord wanted the young man, not his wealth. But as long as the young man had his mind on his riches, he couldn't follow the Lord with freedom. He needed to be free of that.

> 11 *And now I am no longer in the world, but these are in the world, and I come to thee. Holy Father, those whom thou hast given me, keep them in thy name, that they may be one, as we are.*

Many of those who name the name of our Lord here on earth are not *one*, and their testimony is terrible. The fighting and the wars that have been going on down through the ages are quite astonishing. This verse has not been fulfilled yet, but it will be fulfilled.

> 12 *While I was with them in the world, I kept them in thy name; those that thou gavest me I have kept, and none of them is lost, but the son of perdition, that the scripture might be fulfilled.*

> 13 *And now I come to thee; and these things I speak in the world that they might have my joy fulfilled in themselves.*

> 14 *I have given them thy word, and the world has hated them because they are not of the world, even as I am not of the world.*

I ask you to consider all these people who name the name of the Lord and for whom everything is going well in this world, here in this corrupt system; do you suppose they don't belong to the Lord?

They do not, because those who really are the Lord's will go against every injustice and every lie that they see all around them (James 4:4).

15 *I do not pray that thou should take them out of the world, but that thou should keep them from the evil.*

The Lord is not sending us to live in a monastery. He is sending us to be a light here in the middle of much darkness, all the while knowing that many people don't like the light. But as I have said before, the light is not to blind people so badly that they can't see anything. The light is to show the way. If we have the light, if we walk in the light, we can be a good example to the rest of the world. Our job is not to judge anyone; our job is to follow the Lord and seek truth and cleanness in our dealings with everyone.

15 *I do not pray that thou should take them out of the world, but that thou should keep them from the evil.*

16 *They are not of the world, even as I am not of the world.*

17 *Sanctify them in thy truth; thy word is the truth.*

The word *sanctify* here does not mean "make them perform all sort of religious acts and dress in a religious way." The phrase *sanctify them* means "separate them so they can live your truth and not the lie that is so prevalent all around." *To be sanctified* means "to be separated and set apart to be used exclusively by the Lord."

18 *As thou hast sent me into the world, even so have I also sent them into the world.*

19 *And for their sakes I sanctify myself, that they also might be sanctified in the truth.*

What is the Lord saying here? He separates Himself so that from now on (and He made this prayer almost two thousand years ago) He can live in us so we can walk in truth. This is His purpose. This is why

He now has all power and all authority to implement the truth in His life and in ours. If He adjusts us to the truth, we will have cleanness in our hearts and in our minds. And the fruit will be as a result of our lives lived according to His pleasure.

> 20 *Neither do I pray for these alone, but also for those who shall believe in me through their word;*

Here he is talking about us.

> 21 *that they all may be one; as thou, Father, art in me, and I in thee, that they also may be one in us, that the world may believe that thou hast sent me.*

Until now, we haven't seen this, and this is why the world does not believe. The Lord is talking about something much different from any of the world systems. The Lord is talking about a kingdom of God where there is a people of God. If anyone hurts in any part, we all hurt. If anyone is exalted in any part, we are all exalted. Wherever there is a need, we will give of our meager resources to fill that need. And if we have a need, the Lord will also provide.

How will He provide? Through those who are sensitive to the leading of the Lord. It's a sharing process, but Paul also said that he who doesn't work shouldn't eat, because God knows the heart.

> 22 *And the clarity which thou gavest me I have given them, that they may be one, even as we are one:*

> 23 *I in them, and thou in me, that they may be perfect in one and that the world may know that thou hast sent me and hast loved them as thou hast loved me.*

The Lord has given us all the necessary provision, but it will cost us something to receive it. It will cost getting rid of all our corruption. It will cost all our corrupt desires. It will cost all our corrupt thoughts.

And if we are not willing to let go of our desires, we can't receive the provision that He has for us.

> 24 *Father, I will that they also, whom thou hast given me, be with me where I am, that they may behold my clarity, which thou hast given me, for thou hast loved me from before the foundation of the world.*

> 25 *O righteous Father, the world has not known thee; but I have known thee, and these have known that thou hast sent me.*

> 26 *And I have manifested unto them thy name and will manifest it still, that the love with which thou hast loved me may be in them, and I in them.*

In the original, the word *clarity* is used. That clarity is of the life and the love of God. We cannot be one unless we have the life and the nature of God in us, and that is why Jesus came. Until now, the picture of the Lord's church, the people of God, has been that the husbandman wanted a good harvest. He planted good seed, but his enemy came in the night, planted the tares, and mixed everything up.

His servants asked Him, *Wilt thou then that we go and gather them up?* And He said, *No, lest while ye gather up the tares, ye root up also the wheat with them. Let both grow together until the harvest, and in the time of harvest I will say to the reapers, Gather ye together first the tares and bind them in bundles to burn them, but gather the wheat into my barn* (Matthew 13:28-30). And this is what many religious groups don't understand – that the Lord is managing all of this at the end to get rid of the tares, the impure and all the hypocrites from within the true people of God.

The coming events are of such magnitude that only the person who has the life of the Lord in them will have the wisdom, the discernment, and the resources to survive and help others. The world is becoming a more and more dangerous place. Petroleum is running out, and they are fighting over it. Resources are very limited. The economies of the big blocks and companies are at war. Some companies have gained almost as much power as nations, each one with its own interests and its own corruptions.

But the Lord can take us above all of these circumstances because where our treasure is there also is our heart. If our treasure is in the truth and the things of God, these wars and fighting over the corrupt things of this world won't interest us. If we seek first the kingdom of God and His righteousness, the Scripture says in Matthew 6:33 that the Lord will add all the things we need. And we won't have to seek after these things if we are seeking the kingdom of God and His righteousness.

Let's pray.
Lord, we give you thanks for your Word. We ask you, Lord, to give us clarity in our hearts: clarity, transparency, and integrity. We ask, Lord, that we may come out of the world of hypocrisy, out of the corruption of the world to know your grace, your love, and to be able to transmit these to those around us. Amen.

The Plan of God for His Friends – Russell M. Stendal
Original title: "El Plan de Dios para Sus Amigos"
Translated into English by Gloria Stendal

The Truth About Tithing

The Tithe According to the New Covenant

Russell M. Stendal

The Truth About Tithing

The Tithe According to the New Covenant

Russell M. Stendal

LIFE SENTENCE
Publishing, LLC

Tithing

8 *Will a man rob God? Yet ye have robbed me. But ye say, In what have we robbed thee? In the tithes and the offerings.*

9 *Ye are cursed with a curse: for ye, even this whole nation, have robbed me.*

10 *Bring ye all the tithes into the storehouse, and there shall be food in my house, and prove me now in this, saith the LORD of hosts, if I will not open you the windows of heaven and pour you out a blessing that there shall not be room enough to receive it.*

11 *And I will reprehend the devourer for your sakes, and he shall not destroy the fruits of the ground; neither shall the vine in the field abort, said the LORD of hosts.*

12 *And all the Gentiles shall call you blessed: for ye shall be a delightsome land, said the LORD of hosts* (Malachi 3:8-12).

We are all familiar with the above Scripture. Verse 10 is cited with great frequency (just before the offering) in many church services. Yet, exactly what is referred to here by the phrase *all the tithes*? What is the *storehouse*? Why do so many ministers of the gospel tell us one minute that we are *not under the law, but under grace* and in the next minute insist on a legal application of tithing?

Some would answer by saying that Abraham was an example of the practice of tithing before the giving of the Law, when he gave the tithe of the spoils of battle to Melchisedec after the slaughter of the kings. But if this justifies Old Testament tithing in the New Covenant, then what about Old Testament circumcision which was also instituted by Abraham before the giving of the Law? Paul makes it very clear that the circumcision of the New Covenant is the circumcision of the heart, and he warns against those who would force the Gentiles to submit to a legalistic Old Testament application of this truth (Romans 2:26-28; 4:9-12; 1 Corinthians 7:19; Galatians 5:6; Philippians 3:2-3; Colossians 2:11; Titus 1:10).

There are only seven references to tithes in the New Testament (Matthew 23:23; Luke 11:42; 18:12; Hebrews 7:5-6, 8-9). All of these refer to the Old Covenant and not directly to the New Covenant. The three references in the Gospels all coincide in pointing out that the giving of tithes does not qualify a person for the blessing of the New Covenant.

The four verses in Hebrews 7 point out that the Levitical priesthood that received the tithes has been changed to the Melchisedec order of the priesthood of all believers in Christ under the Lord Jesus, and that a change in the priesthood also means a change in the law. Therefore, anyone wishing to implement a legal application of tithing in the church is forced to use Old Testament Scriptures (such as Malachi 3:10) because the New Testament Scriptures focus on tithing from an entirely different angle. There are no recorded examples of tithing (Old Testament style) in the New Testament church in Scripture.

In the King James Bible, the word *tithe* or *tithes* is used in thirty-two verses (twenty-five in the Old Testament and seven in the New Testament). The word *firstfruits* is also used in thirty-two verses (twenty-four in the Old Testament and eight in the New Testament).

In the Old Testament, the firstfruits are part of the tithe. The words *firstfruits* and *tithe* are related or equivalent in many passages (check this out).

In the Old Testament, for two years the tithe was to be taken before the Lord in Jerusalem and:

> 28 *At the end of three years thou shalt bring forth all the tithe of thine increase the same year and shalt lay it up within thy gates:* (Deuteronomy 14:28).

> 12 *When thou hast made an end of tithing all the tithes of thy fruits the third year, which is the year of tithing and hast given it unto the Levite, the stranger, the fatherless, and the widow, that they may eat within thy gates, and be filled* (Deuteronomy 26:12).

I have never heard any of our modern-day clergy teach that every third year each individual should store up their tithe within their own gates and share it with the stranger (the unsaved), the fatherless, and the widow, as well as with the Levite. Also, according to 1 Chronicles 29:5-9, the temple was not constructed with tithe money but with freewill offerings. There is no precedent of any sort in the Old Testament for using tithe money for constructing buildings. And under the New Covenant, there is no example or reference to material buildings at all, period. In the New Covenant we are the temple of the Lord (1 Corinthians 3:16; 2 Corinthians 6:16).

In the New Testament, we are the firstfruits; we are part of the tithe that belongs to the LORD (1 Corinthians 7:23).

> 16 *Do not err, my beloved brethren.*

17 *Every good gift and every perfect gift is from above and comes down from the Father of lights, with whom is no variableness, neither shadow of turning.*

18 *He, of his own will, has begotten us with the word of truth, that we should be the firstfruits of his creatures* (James 1:16-18).

3 *and they sang as it were a new song before the throne and before the four animals and the elders; and no man could learn that song but the hundred and forty-four thousand, who were redeemed from the earth.*

4 *These are those who are not defiled with women, for they are virgins. These are those who follow the Lamb wherever he goes. These are redeemed from among men, being the firstfruits unto God and to the Lamb.*

5 *And in their mouth was found no guile, for they are without blemish before the throne of God* (Revelation 14:3-5).

Under the Old Covenant, we were taught that *thou shalt not kill.* Under the New Covenant, we are taught that *whosoever is angry with his brother out of control shall be in danger of the judgment.*

Under the Old Covenant, we were taught that *thou shalt not commit adultery.* Under the New Covenant, we are taught that *whosoever looks on a woman to lust after her has committed adultery with her already in his heart.*

Under the Old Covenant, we were taught to *Remember the sabbath day, to sanctify it.* Under the New Covenant, we are to enter into His rest every day and desist from our own works. Therefore, Paul writes that we are to let *no one therefore judge you in food or in drink or in respect of a feast day or of the new moon or of the sabbath days, which are a shadow of things to come* (Colossians 2:16-3:5).

Under the Old Covenant we were to give a tithe. Under the New Covenant we are to give ourselves.

Let us take another look at the full context of Malachi 3 in the light of the New Covenant.

17 *Ye* [the modern day church of the Laodiceans] *have wearied the LORD with your words. Yet ye say, In what have we wearied him? When ye say, Every one that does evil pleases the LORD, and he delights in them; or, Where is the God of judgment* [when you trust doctrines and traditions of men rather than the Word of God]?

1 *Behold, I will send my messenger, and he shall prepare the way before me; and the Lord, whom ye seek, shall suddenly come to his temple* [His people], *and the angel of the covenant, whom ye desire: behold, he comes, saith the LORD of the hosts.* [The second coming of the LORD is at hand.]

2 *But who may abide the time of his coming* [the day of the LORD]? *and who shall stand when he appears? for he shall be like a refiner's fire and like fullers' soap* [(2 Peter 3)]:

3 *And he shall sit to refine and to purify the silver: for he shall purify the sons of Levi* [the New Covenant is the priesthood of all believers, a *kingdom of priests*] *and purge them as gold and silver that they may offer unto the LORD an offering in righteousness.*

4 *Then the offering of Judah* [those who praise God] *and Jerusalem* [the city of peace] *shall be pleasant unto the*

LORD as in the days of old and as in former years [as in the early church].

5 *And I will come near unto you for judgment; and I will be a swift witness against the sorcerers* [against the false prophets with religious spirits in the church who build their own kingdoms with tithes and offerings] *and against the adulterers* [those who make promiscuous use of the name of the Lord] *and against false swearers* [those who take the name of the Lord in vain] *and against those* [who run the church like a business franchise] *that oppress the hireling in his wages, the widow, and the fatherless, and that turn aside the stranger* [the unbeliever] *from his right* [to hear a pure message], *and do not fear me, saith the LORD of the hosts.* [The fear of the LORD is sadly lacking in most of the churches today.]

6 *For I am the LORD, I have not changed; therefore, ye sons of Jacob* [Jacob is an unconverted Israel trying to get the inheritance of the kingdom by his own astuteness] *have not been consumed.*

7 *Even from the days of your fathers, ye had departed from my ordinances* [from God's way of doing things] *and had never kept them. Return unto me* [like Jacob did at Peniel when the Angel of God crippled his natural walk in the flesh], *and I will return unto you, saith the LORD of the hosts. But ye said, In what shall we return?*

8 *Will a man rob God? Yet ye have robbed me. But ye say, In what have we robbed thee? In the tithes and the offerings.* [The modern day church has taken the people of God (who

are the tithes which are to be offered unto God under the New Covenant) and enslaved them in the kingdoms of man instead of releasing them into the liberty of the sons of God.]

9 *Ye* [the church] *are cursed with a curse: for ye, even this whole nation, have robbed me* [even every denomination].

10 *Bring ye all the tithes* [all those who are firstfruits unto God and to the Lamb] *into the storehouse* [of a vital, nourishing, personal, hearing relationship with God], *and there shall be food in my house* [Jesus, the bread of life, wants to make us like Himself so that we can be food for the nations], *and prove me now in this, saith the LORD of the hosts, if I will not open you the windows of heaven and pour you out a blessing that there shall not be room enough to receive it.*

11 *And I will reprehend the devourer for your sakes, and he shall not destroy the fruits of the ground* [of the church]; *neither shall the vine in the field abort* [the fruit shall come to maturity], *said the LORD of the hosts.*

12 *And all the Gentiles* [the unconverted] *shall call you blessed: for ye shall be a delightsome land* [of people overflowing with the fruit of the Spirit], *said the LORD of the hosts.*

13 *Your words have prevailed against me, saith the LORD. Yet ye say, What have we spoken against thee?*

14 *Ye have said, It is vain to serve God, and what profit is it that we have kept his law and that we walk mournfully before the LORD of the hosts?*

15 *We say, therefore, now, that blessed are the proud and even that those that work wickedness are prospered; those that tempted God have escaped.* [Those ministers and ministries who have little or no fear of the Lord seem to have obtained great prosperity in the eyes of the world and of much of the church.]

16 *Then those that feared the LORD spoke one to another, and the LORD hearkened and heard it, and a book of remembrance was written before him for those that feared the LORD and for those that think in his name.*

17 *And they shall be mine, said the LORD of the hosts, in that day* [the day of the LORD] *when I make up my jewels; and I will spare them, as a man spares his own son that serves him.*

18 *Therefore become ye converted, and he shall make a difference between the just and the wicked, between him that serves God and him that did not serve him.*

1 *For, behold, the day comes* [the day of the LORD is upon us] *that shall burn as an oven; and all the proud, and all that do wickedly shall be stubble; and the day that comes shall burn them up, said the LORD of the hosts, that it shall leave them neither root nor branch.* [The judgment that begins in the house of the Lord shall leave a clean, purified church without spot or wrinkle ready for the return of our Lord.] (Malachi 2:17-4:1).

It is sad and ironic that many of the very ministers and ministries that zealously preach tithing by laying a religious guilt trip on the people are themselves guilty in God's eyes of the very thing they are warning others about! They warn others about the consequences of robbing God of His tithes and offerings, while they themselves are busy taking the people of God, who are the firstfruits under the New Covenant (the first of the tithe that belongs to God), to themselves for the purpose of building their own kingdoms in God's name.

They make proud and arrogant statements such as, "What do you prefer? Ninety percent (of your income) with blessing or one hundred percent with a curse?" We can't bribe God. He isn't interested in ten percent of our money. He wants us, and if He were to require all of our money, we should give it. But Jesus didn't want the rich young ruler's money for Himself. He told him to give it to the poor. Jesus wanted the rich young ruler himself, who first needed to be delivered from being rich and from being a ruler so he might learn to depend upon God and become a servant.

When someone comes in with a desperate need and the pastor asks the person if they are tithing their income to the church, some pastors refuse to pray for the person if the answer is no. One minister replied and said, "How can I pray for you if you don't tithe to the church? I'm not so anointed that I can bless what God has cursed."

I believe that this dedicated minister is sincerely mistaken. Contrast his statement with Samuel's reply to the people when they became unsure of themselves after they had asked for (and received) King Saul (in the midst of their rebellion against God).

> 23 Moreover as for me, in no wise should I sin against the LORD in ceasing to pray for you, but I will teach you the good and the right way (1 Samuel 12:23).

The good and the right way refers to the LORD alone leading His people (Deuteronomy 32:12). Under the New Covenant, we are to be led by the Spirit of God. Ministry is set in place by God for the purpose of joining the individual to God and diligently watching to make sure that the individual remains joined to the Lord to edify the body of Christ.

The very authority and autonomy of the Spirit of God (the Holy Spirit is the vicar of Christ) is challenged and rebelled against by those who would have the individual blindly pay a tithe into the coffers of their ministry or church instead of encouraging the individual to hear from God on a personal basis in all things including finances. When we hear from God for ourselves, the voice of God, then the personal word of the Lord to us becomes a creative word and enables us to do whatever He tells us if we receive the word with faith. The spoken word of the Lord contains all of the grace, power, and provision necessary for us to victoriously comply with what He says and resist the wiles of the enemy. For *Man shall not live by bread alone, but by every word that proceeds out of the mouth of God* (Matthew 4:4).

When the carnal desire to have a king like the other *denomi-*nations sets in and men begin to yield to the temptation to *make us a name, lest we be scattered,* God has chosen time and time again to yield to the desires of the people while at the same time He admonishes that:

11 *This will be the right of the king that shall reign over you: He will take your sons and appoint them for himself* [he will "father" your sons], *for his chariots, and to be his horsemen, and some shall run before his chariot.*

12 *And he will appoint captains over thousands and captains over fifties* [human organization and bureaucracy will set in] *and will set them to plough his ground and to reap his harvest and to make his weapons of war and munitions of his chariots.* [Man sends forth the workers and warriors instead of God sending them forth into the field of evangelism and into the spiritual battles.]

13 *And he will take your daughters to be confectionaries and to be cooks and to be bakers.* [Man sets up Bible schools and seminaries to cook up all sorts of doctrine inspired by the soul of man.]

14 *And he will take your fields and your vineyards and your good oliveyards and give them to his servants.* [Man distributes the leadership and authority in the churches as if he were running a business franchise.]

15 *And he will take the tenth* [the tithe] *of your seed and of your vineyards to give to his officers and to his servants.*

16 *And he will take your menservants and your maidservants and your good young men and your asses and do his work with them* [instead of God's work].

17 *He will also take the tenth* [the tithe] *of your sheep, and finally ye shall be his servants* [slaves].

18 *And ye shall cry out in that day because of your king which ye shall have chosen you, and the LORD will not hear you in that day* [of unanswered prayers].

19 *Nevertheless, the people refused to hear the voice of Samuel, and they said, No, but we will have a king over us*

20 *that we also may be like all the Gentiles and that our king may govern us and go out before us and fight our battles.*

21 *And Samuel heard all the words of the people, and he rehearsed them in the ears of the LORD.*

22 *And the LORD said to Samuel, Hearken unto their voice, and place a king over them. Then Samuel said unto the men of Israel, Go each one unto his city* (1 Samuel 8:11-22).

When man is king, every man ends up in his own religious city (kingdom). When God is the King, we come into the City of God.

The kingdom of Saul has had its day in the church. The day of man's control is almost over. The day of the Lord is at hand, and the New Covenant will be fulfilled in and through a people who have fully entered into the new priesthood in Christ. Let us look at this in the book of Hebrews:

13 *For when God promised unto Abraham, because he could swear by no greater, he swore by himself,*

14 *saying, Surely blessing I will bless thee and multiplying I will multiply thee.* [How can we tap into this blessing?]

19 *which we have as an anchor of the soul, both sure and steadfast, and which enters even into that which is within the veil* [directly into the presence of God].

20 *where our precursor, Jesus, has entered for us and is made high priest for ever after the order of Melchisedec* (Hebrews 6:13-14, 19-20).

1 *For this Melchisedec, king of Salem, priest of the most high God, who met Abraham returning from the slaughter of the kings* [after delivering Lot and the people of Sodom and Gomorrah] *and blessed him,*

2 *to whom Abraham also gave a tenth part of all* [the goods of Lot and of all that belonged to the kings and to the people of Sodom and Gomorrah]; *first being by interpretation King of righteousness, and after that also King of Salem, which*

is King of peace [the Lord Jesus Christ is the only one who fits this description];

3 *without father, without mother, without lineage, having neither beginning of days, nor end of life, but made like unto the Son of God; abides a priest continually.*

4 *Now consider how great this man was, unto whom even the patriarch Abraham gave the tenth of the spoils.*

5 *And verily those that are of the sons of Levi, who receive the priesthood, have a commandment to take tithes of the people according to the law, that is, of their brethren, though they have come out of the loins of Abraham;*

6 *but he whose descent is not counted in those took tithes from Abraham and blessed him that had the promises.*

7 *And without all contradiction the less is blessed of the better.*

8 *In the same manner, here men that die take tithes; but there he received them, of whom it is witnessed that he lives.*

9 *And as I may so say, Levi also, who received tithes, paid tithes in Abraham.* [It is important to note that Abraham did not receive the tithes; Melchisedec did. Abraham took nothing for himself and waited, a pilgrim and a stranger in the land, for a yet future promise because he had a vision of a city whose builder and maker is God (Genesis 14:22-15:1; Hebrews 11)].

10 *For he was yet in the loins of his father, when Melchisedec met him.*

11 *If therefore perfection were by the Levitical priesthood (for under it the people received the law), what further need was there that another priest should rise after the order of Melchisedec and not be called after the order of Aaron?* [Abraham was perfected by grace through faith, not through law.]

12 *For the priesthood being transposed, there is made of necessity a translation also of the law* [from the law of sin and death to the law of the Spirit of life (Romans 8:2), that we might be judged by the law of liberty (James 1:25; 2:12)].

13 *For he of whom these things are spoken pertains to another tribe, of which no one presided at the altar.*

14 *For it is evident that our Lord sprang out of Juda of which tribe Moses spoke nothing concerning priesthood.*

15 *And it is yet far more manifest: if there arises another priest who is like unto Melchisedec,*

16 *who is not made according to the law of a carnal commandment, but by the power of an indissoluble* [or eternal] *life;*

17 *for the testimony is of this manner, Thou art a priest for ever after the order of Melchisedec.*

18 *For there is verily a disannulling of the commandment going before* [including the Old Testament tithe] *for the weakness and unprofitableness of it;*

19 *for the law made nothing perfect* [Matthew 23:23; Luke 11:42 and 18:12 make it clear that tithing under law could not bring anyone into the blessing of the New Covenant],

but the bringing in of a better hope did, by which we draw near unto God [if we offer ourselves unto God – through the high priestly ministration of the Lord Jesus Christ – we can draw nigh boldly unto the throne of grace].

20 *And even more, inasmuch as it is not without an oath*

21 *(for the others indeed without an oath were made priests, but this one with an oath by him that said unto him, The Lord swore and will not repent, Thou art a priest for ever after the order of Melchisedec);*

22 *by so much better testament* [under which we are the firstfruits or the first part of the tithe that is to be given unto Him] *is Jesus made surety.*

23 *And the others, truly, were many priests because they were not able to continue by reason of death:*

24 *but this man, because he continues forever, has the intransmissible priesthood.*

25 *Therefore he is able also to save to the uttermost those that come unto God by him, seeing he ever lives to make intercession for them.*

26 *For it was expedient that we have such a high priest, who is holy, innocent, undefiled, separate from sinners, and made higher than the heavens,*

27 *who needs not daily, as those high priests, to offer up sacrifice, first for his own sins and then for the people's; for this he did once, when he offered up himself.*

28 *For the law makes men high priests who have weakness;
but the word of the oath, which was after the law, has made
perfect a Son forever* (Hebrews 7:1-28).

1 *Now of the things which we have spoken, this is the sum:
We have such a high priest who sat down at the right hand
of the throne of the Majesty in the heavens,*

2 *a minister of the sanctuary and of the true tabernacle,
which the Lord pitched, and not man* [take note that there
is a true house and an imitation house].

3 *For every high priest is ordained to offer gifts and sacrifices;
therefore, it is also necessary that this one have somewhat
also to offer.*

4 *For if he were on earth, he should not even be a priest,
being present still the other priests that offer gifts according
to the law,*

5 *(who serve as an example and shadow of the heavenly things,
as Moses was admonished of God when he was about to make
the tabernacle: for, See, saith he, that thou make all things
according to the pattern showed unto thee in the mount);*

6 *but now a more excellent ministry is his, in that he is the
mediator of a better testament, which was established upon
better promises.*

7 *For if that first covenant had been faultless, then no place
should have been sought for the second.*

8 *For finding fault with them* [with those under the law],
he said, Behold, the days come, saith the Lord, when I will

make a new testament with the house of Israel and with the house of Judah,

9 not according to the testament that I made with their fathers in the day when I took them by the hand to lead them out of the land of Egypt, because they did not continue in my testament, and I regarded them not, saith the Lord.

10 For this is the testament that I will ordain to the house of Israel after those days, saith the Lord: I will give my laws into their soul and write them upon their hearts, and I will be to them a God, and they shall be to me a people:

11 and no one shall teach his neighbour nor anyone his brother, saying, Know the Lord, for all shall know me, from the least to the greatest [and this is still not the case].

12 For I will reconcile their iniquities and their sins, and their iniquities I will remember no more.

13 In that he says, New, he has made the first old. Now that which decays and waxes old is ready to vanish away (Hebrews 8:1-13).

Throughout this present age of the church, man has clung tenaciously to elements of the decayed Old Covenant and has not allowed them to *vanish away*. Man has divided the priesthood of all believers into clergy and laity. In many cases, the clergy have come between the people and God, interrupting and even usurping the role of the Holy Spirit who is the vicar of Christ on the earth (John 14:15-18; 16:12-15). Therefore, the promise of verse 11 above has not yet become a reality in the church. When man usurps the leadership of God, man invariably focuses on money instead of on mercy (verse 12).

Paul wrote Timothy that *the love of money is the root of all evil* (1 Timothy 6:6-12). When the love of money begins to infiltrate the ministry under the guise of "Think of the wonderful outreach we could have if we could only get these people to tithe," or "For every ten tithers we can support a full-time minister or missionary," or "If our people would only tithe, we could build a larger sanctuary (storehouse)," then the root of all evil gets mixed in with all the seemingly noble intentions. Within a few years (or a generation at most), those who go this route invariably find themselves alienated from the mercy of God in a church that is now spiritually dead or dying even in the midst of financial prosperity.

The love of money, which is the root of all evil and which insidiously refuses to relinquish the Old Testament doctrine of Levitical tithing, is diametrically opposed to the fear of the LORD which is the beginning of wisdom. The fear of the LORD is the only thing that will restore the true blessing of God to His people instead of the curse described in Malachi 3:9 (the actual state of most of the church). For *the mercy of the LORD is from everlasting to everlasting upon those that fear him* (Psalm 103:11, 13, 17).

When we understand that we are the tithe, the firstfruits unto God and to the Lamb, then it follows that everything that belongs to us must be put at the feet of the Lord and administered according to the leading of the Holy Spirit. Instead of ten tithers supporting one full-time minister Old Testament style, under the New Covenant, *one [could] chase a thousand, and two put ten thousands to flight!* (Deuteronomy 32:30).

The promises of the New Covenant have been delayed in their fulfillment due to man's pride and arrogance, but they shall be fulfilled because the Word of the Lord shall not return void. It is important that we understand that God's promises are conditional and that the blessings of the New Covenant will not be released by fulfilling the conditions of the Old Covenant. Under the New Testament, sealed with the blood of Jesus Christ, it is not a tithe of our worldly goods that qualifies us for the blessing, but rather we must be crucified with Christ if we are to enter into the blessing of the life of faith (Galatians 2:20). We must place ourselves on the altar of God and remain there as living sacrifices if we are to be transformed by the power of God (Romans 12:1-2).

God knew that man would always prefer to remain under a covenant of law instead of under one of grace, so he made provision for the time of the end:

> 28 *when the consumption comes to an end, righteousness shall overflow, because a short sentence will the Lord execute upon the earth* (Romans 9:28).

Here Paul is actually quoting Isaiah 10:22 (the translation here, via Greek into English, comes out slightly different than the original). Isaiah 10 starts out like this:

> 1 *Woe unto those that establish unrighteous laws and that willfully prescribe tyranny* [woe unto them who turn the covenant of grace into one of law (Matthew 23)].

> 2 *to turn aside the poor from right judgment and to take away the right from the afflicted of my people that widows may be their prey and that they may rob the fatherless!*

> 3 *And what will ye do in the day of visitation and in the desolation which shall come from far? To whom will ye flee for help and where will ye leave your glory?* (Isaiah 10:1-3).

Under the Old Covenant, the tithes were to feed the needy, the widows, the fatherless, and the stranger, in addition to the Levites.

Under the New Covenant, we are the provision of God for the needy of the world. The idea that we can pay one-tenth of our income to the church of our choice and then spend the remaining ninety percent any fool way we please is from the enemy.

If we can be lured back under the law of sin and death, the Devil is the clear beneficiary. The New Covenant is a TOTAL commitment so that we might enter into the law of the Spirit of life (Romans 8:2), that we might be judged by the law of liberty (James 1:25; 2:12).

In the early church, they sold their possessions and gave everything. One exception to this is mentioned for our edification: Ananias and Sapphira sold some property and pretended to give all, while they secretly kept a little bit back for themselves. Maybe they gave ninety percent and kept ten percent. After they both fell down dead before Peter for attempting to deceive the Holy Spirit, the Scripture says that great fear of the LORD fell on the entire church and on everyone who heard the story (Acts 5:1-11).

Isaiah 10 prophesies this same sort of thing for the day of the Lord at the time of the end. Here is the context regarding the portion that Paul quoted in Romans 9:28:

> 21 *The remnant shall become converted, even the remnant of Jacob, unto the mighty God.*
>
> 22 *For though thy people Israel be as the sand of the sea* [Abraham was promised two kinds of descendants, natural ones *as the sands of the sea* and spiritual ones *as the stars of the heaven* (Genesis 15:5; 22:17; 26:4; 32:12)], *yet the remnant of them shall become converted; when the consumption comes to an end, righteousness shall overflow* [the judgment of God is upon the natural man that He might bring forth the spiritual man].

23 *For the Lord GOD of the hosts shall make a consumption* [total judgment] *and an end in the midst of all the land* [the people of God] (Isaiah 10:21-23).

The judgment that begins in the house of the LORD is clarified even more in Isaiah 28.

1 *Woe to the crown of pride, to the drunkards of Ephraim* [Ephraim means double fruitfulness, here applied to those mentioned in Malachi 3:15] *and to the open flower of the beauty of their glory* [Isaiah 40:6-8; 2 Peter 1:17-21] *which is upon the head of the fertile valley of those that are overcome with wine* [drunk on the power that they wield over the people of God]!

2 *Behold, the Lord has a mighty and strong one* [the true body of Christ of which the Lord Jesus is the head] *who as a tempest of hail and a destroying storm, as a flood of mighty waters overflowing shall cast down to the earth with the hand.* [Up until now in the age of grace, the age of Pentecost, the Word has fallen as the rain, the *early rain* and the *latter rain* which waters (prospers) all the seeds of the garden (good or bad). Now, at the beginning of the day of the Lord, the Word will fall like hail and lightning (Exodus 9:18-26; Revelation 8:7)].

3 *The crown of pride, the drunkards of Ephraim, shall be trodden under feet:*

4 *And the fading flower of the beauty of their glory, which is upon the head of the fertile valley, shall be as the early fig, which comes first before the other fruits of the summer; which*

when he that looks upon it sees it; as soon as he has it is in his hand, he eats it up.

5 In that day the LORD of the hosts shall be for a crown of glory and for a diadem of beauty unto the residue of his people,

6 And for a spirit of judgment to him that sits upon the throne of judgment, and for strength to those that turn the battle to the gate.

7 But they also have erred through wine, and through strong drink are out of the way; the priest and the prophet have erred through strong drink; they are swallowed up of wine, they are out of the way through strong drink; they err in vision, they stumble in judgment. [The headiness of the kingdoms of man within the church has taken its toll among the "priests" and the "prophets," producing a terrible hangover in the end.]

8 For all tables are full of vomit and filthiness, so that there is no place clean. [This is what the kingdoms of man with all the ornate cathedrals, chapels, ministries, installations, and institutions look like now in the eyes of God.]

9 Whom shall he teach knowledge? and whom shall he make to understand doctrine? Those that are weaned from the milk and drawn from the breasts.

10 For precept must be upon precept, precept upon precept; line upon line, line upon line; here a little, and there a little [we must be weaned from the church of man if we are to mature in the Lord]:

11 *For with stammering lips and another tongue he will speak to this people* [in the language of the Spirit (1 John 2:27)].

12 *To whom he said, This is the rest with which ye may cause the weary to rest; and this is the refreshing: yet they would not hear.* [He is the rest, and He is the refreshing, and He remains outside the door of the *church of the Laodiceans* knocking to see if they will let Him in (Revelation 3:14-22).]

13 *But the word of the LORD shall be unto them precept upon precept, precept upon precept; line upon line, line upon line; here a little, and there a little; that they might go and fall backward and be broken and snared and taken.* [Judas fell over backwards at the presence of the Lord; John fell on his face as though dead. Today both options are still viable.]

14 *Therefore hear the word of the LORD, ye scornful men, that have taken rule over this people which is in Jerusalem.*

15 *Because ye have said, We have made a covenant with death, and with Sheol are we at agreement* [those who think that their doctrine will save them]; *when the overflowing scourge shall pass through, it shall not come unto us: for we have made lies our refuge, and under falsehood have we hid ourselves:* [Our doctrine cannot save us even if it is true, much less if it is false. Only Jesus Christ as sovereign Lord can save us.]

16 *Therefore thus saith the Lord GOD, Behold, I lay in Zion for a foundation a stone, a tried stone, a precious corner stone, a sure foundation:* [Jesus Christ as the only LORD and MASTER is that cornerstone and woe to those who reject Him by placing doctrines or traditions in His place]

he that believes [in total commitment] *shall not make hast.* [He shall stand firm and victorious and not have to flee from anyone or anything in the evil day.]

17 *Judgment also will I lay to the line and righteousness to the plummet: and the hail* [of the true Word] *shall sweep away the refuge of lies, and the waters* [of judgment] *shall overflow the hiding place.*

18 *And your covenant with death shall be disannulled, and your agreement with Sheol shall not stand; when the overflowing scourge shall pass through, then ye shall be trodden down by it.*

19 *From the time that it goes forth, it shall take you: for it shall come suddenly, by day and by night: and it shall be that the terror only causes one to understand the report.*

20 *For the bed is shorter than that a man can stretch himself on it* [there is no peace for the wicked]: *and the covering narrower than that he can wrap himself in it.* [Woe to the sons that leave, saith the LORD, to make counsel, but not of me; to cover themselves with a covering, and not by my spirit, adding sin unto sin (Isaiah 30:1).]

21 *For the LORD shall rise up as in Mount Perazim, he shall be wroth as in the valley of Gibeon, that he may do his work, his strange work; and bring to pass his act, his strange act* [as when Joshua commanded the sun to stand still.]

22 *Now therefore be ye not mockers lest your bands be made strong: for I have heard from the Lord GOD of the hosts that consumption and destruction are determined upon the whole earth* (Isaiah 28:1-22).

It is interesting to note that the very first time that the word *tenth* (the root for the word *tithe*) is used in Scripture, it is at the end of the judgment of the world by the flood.

> 5 *And the waters decreased continually until the tenth month;*
> *in the tenth month, on the first day of the month, the tops of*
> *the mountains were seen* (Genesis 8:5).

The tithe, or firstfruits unto the Lord, is represented by the use of the word *tenth* throughout Scripture. Here the *tops of the mountains* are the first thing seen after the judgment. They are seen in the tenth month. This is prophetic also of the judgment by fire at the time of the end, during which the first thing that is seen are one hundred and forty-four thousand standing with the Lamb on Mount Sion, having the Father's name written on their foreheads. The tenth or tithe is prophetic of the true remnant of the redeemed all through the Bible.

The word *tithe* is used in thirty-two verses in the King James Bible, and the word *tenth* is used in sixty-eight verses (one hundred verses all together, which is symbolic of the plan of God). The word *firstfruits* is also used in thirty-two verses in Scripture, and the firstfruits are part of the tithe. The meanings of the two words overlap somewhat.

If we add up the occurrences of all three words (*tithe, tenth,* and *firstfruits*), the total is one hundred thirty-two or two times sixty-six. Sixty-six is the number that is symbolic of the Word of God (there are sixty-six books in the Bible), and two speaks of a corporate body separated unto God. One hundred thirty-two, therefore, is symbolic of the Word of God becoming a reality in a corporate body (the body of Christ). This is the bottom line. This is the true meaning of the tithe under the New Covenant: That we might be *redeemed from among men, being the firstfruits unto God and to the Lamb* (Revelation 14:4).

The sixty-seventh verse in the Bible to use the word *tenth* is found in Revelation.

> 13 *And in the same hour was there a great earthquake, and the tenth part of the city fell* [this is the tithe, or remnant that belongs to the Lord and is taken by Him], *and in the earthquake were slain the names of seven thousand men;* [The original literally says that *the personal names of seven thousand were slain.* This is the prophetic fulfillment of the seven thousand in 1 Kings 19:18 that did not bow the knee to Baal.] *and the others were frightened and* [the fear of the Lord is returned to the city of God so that they] *gave glory to the God of heaven* [instead of taking it for themselves like so many in our modern church of the Laodiceans] (Revelation 11:13).

A name is equivalent to nature in Scripture. From the beginning, everything was named according to its nature. If we are to come forth in the name (nature) of God, then our own name (our old nature) has to die. When we become the tithe that is given completely over unto God, when we become the firstfruits unto God and to the Lamb, then He can eradicate our old nature and write the name of God upon our foreheads so we can stand on Mount Sion with the Lamb.

Final Thoughts

Abraham and Lot are also types and shadows of that which is spiritually represented by *firstfruits* and *tithes* (Genesis 14-19). After the separation of Abraham and Lot, when Abraham chose the high ground, and Lot chose the low, fertile valley of the cities of Sodom (Genesis 13:10-13), Lot (along with the people of Sodom and Gomorrah) was taken captive by four kings.

Abraham, with his 318 servants, came to the rescue and saved Lot and the people of Sodom and Gomorrah, recovering all of their goods (Genesis 14:14-16). Next, the king of Sodom came out to meet Abraham, and in the context of this meeting, Melchisedec appears in the scene and blesses Abraham (he was called Abram at that time). After receiving the blessing, Abraham *gave him [Melchisedec] tithes of all* (Genesis 14:20).

Note here that the blessing came before the tithes were given. Note that the tithes were not *paid*; they were *given* (reflecting free will or grace instead of law). Also note that the tithes were of the spoils of battle that in reality were the goods of Lot and the people of Sodom and Gomorrah.

The end result of all of this was that Lot and the inhabitants of Sodom and Gomorrah were saved by God through Abraham (Genesis 14:19-20), and the tithes of all the goods of Lot and the people of Sodom and Gomorrah were voluntarily given by Abraham to Melchisedec (who is the Lord Jesus Christ according to Hebrews 7) after Abraham received the blessing.

The salvation that God ministered unto the people of Sodom and Gomorrah (who are symbolic of the religious world) through Abraham did not last very long because they failed to walk in it. Only Lot, in his righteous heart, felt bad as he witnessed their sin and perversion. Sodom, the home of Lot, is equated in typology with religious Jerusalem: *the great city, which spiritually is called Sodom and Egypt, where also our Lord was crucified* (Revelation 11:8).

Right about the time that Isaac, the promised manchild, was conceived, the judgment of Sodom was in progress (Genesis 18). Abraham interceded for Sodom and convinced the LORD to spare the city if He found ten righteous men in it (Genesis 18:32). When God visited the city, He only found one man with a righteous heart, Lot. God only found a tithe of what would have been required to save the city. He only found Lot instead of the ten righteous men that Abraham was confident were there. Lot became the tithe that was taken by the LORD from the city of Sodom just before it was totally and eternally destroyed by the judgment of God (in type and shadow this lines up with Revelation 11:13 regarding the judgment of the city of religion).

The fact that the men of Sodom had been saved by God on a previous occasion and had paid the tithe of all their material goods (through the ministry of Abraham) unto Melchisedec (Christ), still did not save them from being consumed in the judgment of God when the time came for God Himself to visit their city. Their conduct toward the angels of God was clearly evil (Genesis 19:5). This same scene was repeated in substance during the first coming of the Lord Jesus Christ to Jerusalem (resulting in the total destruction of the city in AD 70) and could be repeated regarding the entire world at the time of the second coming which is very near. The outcome of this is still to be determined (Malachi 4:6).

Looking at all of this from a slightly different angle, if Sodom also represents the natural man (the man of sin) which must be completely destroyed by the appearing of the Lord, then Lot would represent the soul that God wants to save. Even so, the soul must be brought into submission to the LORD and dealt with. It must be restored and brought to maturity by the Holy Spirit in the New Man (Christ) if it is to become fruitful and multiply and inherit the promise to reign and rule with Him.

At the time of the end, God will use a firstfruits company for the ministry of deliverance and intercession just as He used Abraham in the example cited above. God will also take His *tithe* unto Himself (of all that are truly His) out of the city of religion as the final judgment falls on our present-day, apostate church, just as He removed righteous Lot from Sodom.

There is another major difference between Abraham and Lot that is not readily apparent. The seed of Abraham (Christ) is to inherit the promise. This seed (the many-membered body of Christ with the Lord Jesus as the head) is to be as the stars of the heaven. These are the meek that shall inherit the earth (Matthew 5:5).

On the other hand, the seed of the sons of Lot are not to enter into the congregation of the Lord even unto the tenth generation.

> 2 *A bastard shall not enter into the congregation of the LORD; even to his tenth generation shall he not enter into the congregation of the LORD.*

> 3 *An Ammonite or Moabite* [descendants of the sons of the incestuous daughters of Lot] *shall not enter into the congregation of the LORD; even to their tenth generation*

shall they not enter into the congregation of the LORD for
ever (Deuteronomy 23:2-3).

There are many today who claim the church as their mother, but
God is not their father. The daughters of Lot provided their own father
instead of trusting God to replace their husbands who perished in
the destruction of Sodom (the young men who thought Lot and the
angels were joking when they tried to warn them).

There are many in the church today who have been *fathered* by
righteous men, who have been separated unto God and delivered
from the city of religion, even as Lot was separated and delivered
from Sodom. Yet this will not fully qualify them to enter into the true
congregation of the Lord. Those who are truly fathered by God must
be disciplined, corrected, and chastised directly by God (see Hebrews
12:6-7). Ezekiel writes about a Levitical priesthood that will not be
allowed to come into the presence of God. Only the sons of Zadok
of the order of Mel-chisedec (in Hebrew sedec is the same as Zadoc)
will be allowed to minister unto the Lord.

> 4 *Then brought he me toward the north gate in front of the*
> *house: and I looked, and, behold, the glory of the LORD*
> *filled the house of the LORD; and I fell upon my face* [the
> glory of the LORD is about to be restored to His true house
> and this will cause His true servants to fall on their faces
> before Him].
>
> 5 *And the LORD said unto me, Son of man, pay attention,*
> *and behold with thine eyes and hear with thine ears all that*
> *I say unto thee concerning all the ordinances of the house of*
> *the LORD* [the ways of the LORD] *and all its laws; and pay*
> *attention to the entering in of the house and to every going*
> *forth from the sanctuary* [learn to walk in the Spirit].

6 *And thou shalt say to the rebellious, even to the house of Israel, Thus hath the Lord GOD said: O ye house of Israel, let all your abominations cease.*

7 *In that ye have brought into my sanctuary strangers, uncircumcised in heart and uncircumcised in flesh to be in my sanctuary to pollute it, even my house, when ye offer my bread, the fat and the blood, and they have broken my covenant because of all your abominations* [you have changed the New Covenant into another Old Covenant, bringing the curse of the law upon the church instead of the blessing of Abraham].

8 *And ye have not kept the charge of my holy things; but ye have set keepers of my charge in my sanctuary for yourselves* [taking tithes and offerings unto yourselves].

9 *Thus hath the Lord GOD said; No son of a stranger, uncircumcised in heart nor uncircumcised in flesh shall enter into my sanctuary, of any sons of strangers that are among the children of Israel.* [No one still under the control of the flesh or of the soul shall enter into the true spiritual sanctuary of the restored house.]

10 *And the Levites that are gone away far from me, when Israel went astray, which went astray away from me after their idols; they shall even bear their iniquity* [they must die to their own ways].

11 *Yet they shall be ministers in my sanctuary, gatekeepers at the gates of the house, and servants in the house; they shall slay the burnt offering and the sacrifice for the people, and they shall stand before them to serve them.* [This is similar to

the Gibeonites, the Nethinims (Joshua 9; 1 Chronicles 9:2) who started out with deception and became the woodcutters and water bearers for the tabernacle and later the temple.]

12 *Because they served them before their idols and caused the house of Israel to fall into iniquity; therefore I have lifted up my hand regarding them, saith the Lord GOD, that they shall bear their iniquity* [they must die to their own soulish ways and desires].

13 *And they shall not come near unto me, to serve me as priests, nor to come near to any of my holy things, to my most holy things: but they shall bear their shame and their abominations which they have committed.*

14 *But I will make them keepers of the charge of the house for all the service thereof and for all that shall be done therein* [they shall do the menial labor].

15 *But the priests the Levites, the sons of Zadok* [meaning righteousness; from the same root as Melchi-sedec], *that kept the charge of my sanctuary when the sons of Israel went astray from me* [when the people of God went after the prosperity of this world like Lot], *they* [of the Melchisedec order] *shall come near to me to minister unto me, and they shall stand before me to offer unto me the fat and the blood, saith the Lord GOD:*

16 *They shall enter into my sanctuary, and they shall come near to my table, to minister unto me, and they shall keep my charge* (Ezekiel 44:4-16).

Ministry is a serious responsibility. Those who have been placed in ministry by God and are allowed to touch the tithes and offerings of the LORD are responsible before Him to be faithful (many of the parables of the Lord Jesus relate to this). Consider the case of righteous Lot and of the Levites (ordained by God into the ministry) who did not qualify to inherit the promise. *And if the righteous are saved with difficulty, where shall the unfaithful and the sinner appear?* (1 Peter 4:18). What about those who are soliciting tithes and offerings and have been placed in the ministry by man instead of by God?

> 30 *And all the tithes of the land, whether of the seed of the land or of the fruit of the tree, is the LORD'S: it is holiness unto the LORD* (Leviticus 27:30).

The fear of the LORD is sadly lacking today among most of the people of God, but it is about to be restored. A small remnant is being dealt with and perfected that they might be an example and a ministry unto the rest of the people of God. Yes, God is restoring His house and it will be glorious.

> 6 *And I heard him speaking unto me out of the house; and the man stood by me.*

> 7 *And he said unto me, Son of man, this is the place of my throne* [or authority], *and the place of the soles of my feet* [of those whom I have truly sent], *in which I will dwell in the midst of the sons of Israel for ever, and my holy name, the house of Israel* [those who are called by My name] *shall no longer defile, neither they, nor their kings* [their self-rule], *by their whoredom* [promiscuous use of My name, gifts, and revelation to build their own kingdoms], *nor by the carcasses of their kings* [dead works and abominations of self] *in their altars* [in the kingdoms they have erected where they call the people to worship in My name but according to their own ways].

8 *In their setting of their threshold by my threshold* [they make the people think they are entering My kingdom when in reality they are entering a man-made kingdom], *and their post by my post* [God's posts or columns are called Jaquim (the LORD establishes) and Boaz (only in Him is there strength); man's posts are called "we will establish" and "in us is strength" (2 Chronicles 3:17)], *and a wall between me and them* [there is an insurmountable wall between these two positions], *they have even defiled my holy name by their abominations that they have committed* [by using the gifts of power and revelation from God in such a promiscuous manner according to the whims of self, that it has brought great dishonor to His name even before the heathen]; *therefore I have consumed them in my anger.*

9 *Now let them put away their whoredom* [no man can serve two masters], *and the carcasses of their kings* [the dead works of their selfish abominations], *far from me, and I will dwell in the midst of them for ever* [note that this verse is conditional].

10 *Thou son of man, show this* [true and undefiled] *house to the* [defiled] *house of* [spiritual] *Israel* [that man has built in My name calling it My church] *that they may be ashamed of their iniquities; and let them understand the pattern* [Jesus Christ as sovereign LORD is that pattern].

11 *And if they are ashamed of all that they have done, show them the form of the house* [how God joins His true people together], *and its pattern* [God's purpose for mankind], *and the goings out thereof, and the comings in thereof* [the true liberty and freedom of being dead to sin and alive in

Christ], *and all its figures* [everything that has to be dealt with in us so that we can truly be free in Christ], *and all its descriptions* [God's way of doing things], *and all its paintings,* [all the aspects of walking in the glorious inheritance of the sons of God], *and all its laws* [the law of the Spirit of life (Romans 8:2); the law of liberty (James 1:25; 2:12)]: *and write it in their sight that they may keep the whole form thereof* [that they may be patterned after Jesus Christ] *and all the ordinances thereof* [that they may learn His ways] *and do them* (Ezekiel 43:6-11).

THE TABERNACLE OF DAVID

A Direct Intimate Relationship with God

RUSSELL M. STENDAL

The Tabernacle of David

A direct, intimate, relationship with God

Russell Stendal

LIFE SENTENCE
Publishing, LLC

The Tabernacle of David

I will return, and will restore the tabernacle of David, which is fallen down (Acts 15:16).

At the council of Jerusalem recorded in Acts 15, a great controversy arose regarding the Gentiles who had been converted under the ministry of Paul. Until then, the manner in which the Gentiles were received was determined according to the law of Moses, which included submission to the rite of circumcision and keeping the law of the old covenant.

But Paul had received Gentiles into the Israel of God without circumcision of the flesh and without charging them to keep the law of Moses. This caused a great uproar among the Jews and was the motive behind their persecution of Paul. Even among the Christian Jews in Jerusalem, many felt that the Gentile believers should be circumcised.

Paul believed that the entrance of the Gentiles into the Israel of God (the true people of God) was through Jesus the Christ under a New Covenant in His blood. He preached circumcision of the heart (Colossians 2) by means of a covenant sealed in baptism in water and in the Holy Spirit to enter into the body of the Lord Jesus Christ through repentance and faith. This baptism represents our identification into the death and resurrection of Christ and a willingness to die to ourselves so that the victorious life of Jesus can flow through us by means of the Holy Spirit. Paul preached that there was a new and higher law: *for the law of the Spirit of life in Christ Jesus has made me free from the law of sin and death* (Romans 8:2).

The controversy continued until, after hearing the testimony of Peter concerning his vision and the outpouring of the Holy Spirit on the household of Cornelius, the apostle James powerfully resolved the debate in favor of Paul and Peter by citing a seemingly obscure Scripture from the prophet Amos:

> 13 *Men and brethren, hearken unto me:*
>
> 14 *Simeon has declared how God first visited the Gentiles, to take out of them a people for his name.*
>
> 15 *And to this agree the words of the prophets; as it is written,*
>
> 16 *After this I will return, and will restore the tabernacle of David, which is fallen down; and I will repair its ruins, and I will set it up again:*
>
> 17 *that the men that are left behind might seek after the Lord, and all the Gentiles, upon whom my name is called, saith the Lord, who doeth all these things.*
>
> 19 *Therefore my sentence is that those from among the Gentiles who are converted to God not be troubled,*
>
> 20 *but that we write unto them, that they abstain from pollutions of idols, and from fornication, and from things strangled, and from blood* (Acts 15:13-17; 19-20; Amos 9).

What was this Tabernacle of David? Why were these dogmatic Jews (some were Pharisees) convinced by such a strange argument (v. 28)?

When David failed to bring the ark of God home (to Jerusalem) in the *new cart,* causing the death of Uzzah (the strong man) and the *breach* God made upon his people, he learned his lesson. The next time they brought the ark (the anointing and the glory) of God *according to due order* upon the shoulders of the Levites sanctified for this purpose (1 Chronicles 15:11-15).

But when they arrived in Jerusalem, instead of restoring the ark to the Tabernacle (which still existed in Shiloh) according to the requirements of the law of Moses, David pitched a simple tent in the backyard of his house and put it there! They placed the ark of the glory of God in a common tent without an intermediary priest, without furniture, without a holy place, without a bronze altar, and without continual blood sacrifices. And David entered this tent frequently to have communion with God without any religious rites or rituals whatsoever!

In the Tabernacle that God ordered Moses to make, all the rites and rituals had to be kept to perfection for a whole year, and only one man, the high priest, could enter the Holy of Holies of the presence of God for a few moments once a year. Any carelessness could produce the death of the high priest, whose dead body would then have to be removed from the Holy of Holies by a rope previously tied around his ankle – to protect the lives of the other priests who could not enter the Holy of Holies under any circumstances.

The raising up of the Tabernacle of David is a perfect picture of the intimate and personal communion that all who have died to their own ways enter into the Way of the *greater son of David* and enjoy uninterrupted fullness with God the Father without any need for an intermediary clergy, religious rites, structures, organizations, or denominations. The simple tent or tabernacle symbolizes our union with Him, and the ark of God symbolizes our access to the glory, unction, and presence of God the Father.

We do not know much about the material design of the Tabernacle of David. God did not see fit to mention the dimensions, the type of materials, or the floor plan of this simple tent that David erected in his backyard. But the apostle Paul resolved the controversy of the council of Jerusalem regarding what should be the model for receiving the Gentiles into the Israel of God. He left no question in the minds of all who were present that day. In Acts 15, before all of the assembly of brothers, elders, and apostles, it is clear that the controversy was resolved; *for it seemed good to the Holy Ghost and to us* that the model for the age of the Gentiles is the Tabernacle of David.

In 1 Chronicles 16:1, when it says *So they brought the ark of God and set it in the midst of the tent that David had pitched for it,* the word *tent* (in Hebrew, *Ohel*) is the word for a simple tent or covering. But when God, through the prophet Amos, speaks of *In that day will I raise up the tabernacle of David that is fallen and close up its breaches; and I will raise up its ruins, and I will build it as in the days of old: that those who are called by my name may possess the remnant of Edom and all the Gentiles* (Amos 9:11-12), the word *tabernacle* (in Hebrew, *cukkah*) is used in the feminine gender and is identical to the word used in Leviticus 23 for *Feast of Tabernacles*. This speaks to us of the bride of Christ under His covering and in the fullness of communion with His Father.

Throughout the long history of the church, men have searched in vain to discover the ideal model for the corporate structure of the church. No hierarchy is clearly spelled out in the Scriptures except what the Spirit says through Paul in the letter to the Corinthians or the Ephesians or in similar Scriptures that say: *But I would have you know that the head of every man is Christ, and the head of the woman is the man, and the head of Christ is God* (1 Corinthians 11:3); and *submitting yourselves one to another in the fear of God* (Ephesians

5:21); and of course, *he gave some, apostles; and some, prophets; and some, evangelists; and some, pastors and teachers; for the perfecting of the saints in the work of the ministry, unto the edifying of the body of Christ until we all come forth in the unity of the faith and of the knowledge of the Son of God unto a perfect man* [unto maturity], *unto the measure of the coming of age of the Christ* (Ephesians 4:11-13).

And the great apostle to the Gentiles said, *be ye followers* [in Greek, imitators] *of me, even as I also am of Christ.* The ministry of the Tabernacle of David exists to join others to Christ and to exhort each and every one to enter into vital and intimate communion with God like David. This ministry also warns others when their communion with God has been broken, and they have lost the ability to personally hear from God (as when Nathan the prophet was sent by God to David to reprove him of his sin with Bathsheba). The Tabernacle of David is the model of the priesthood of all believers.

The New Testament contains many examples of what seemed good to the Holy Spirit at a certain time and place and situation: God named Paul as apostle to the Gentiles without consulting the apostles in Jerusalem; everyone lived in community with all things in common in Jerusalem from AD 33 to about AD 70; and the apostle Paul named elders and deacons in certain places or gave instructions to Timothy or Titus regarding this.

All these examples are of value to us, but only by means of vital and individual contact with Jesus and His Father through the Holy Spirit will we receive wisdom and power to face the situations of today. This is the model of the Tabernacle of David. If we try to repeat what God did in the past when He is no longer doing the same thing today (and God never repeats himself exactly), we will end up in another old order of the letter that kills instead of being ruled by the freedom of the law of the Spirit of life in Christ Jesus.

In the Tabernacle of David, a fundamental change occurs in the priesthood.

11 *If therefore perfection were by the Levitical priesthood* [under a clergical class placed between the people and God] *(for under it the people received the law)* [for many have received instruction in the precepts of God from human ministry], *what further need was there that another priest should rise after the order of Melchisedec* [of Christ and the priesthood of all believers who form part of Him], *and not be called after the order of Aaron* [the order of the authority of God delegated in a clergy class]?

12 *For the priesthood being transposed, there is made of necessity a translation also of the law* (Hebrews 7:11-12).

12 *So speak ye and so do as those that shall be judged by the law of liberty.*

13 *For judgment without mercy shall be done unto the one that has showed no mercy; and mercy boasts against judgment* (James 2:12-13).

The Law of Liberty: To Walk in the Spirit

Under the law of liberty: *ye have been called unto liberty; only do not use liberty for an occasion to the flesh* (Galatians 5:13). But there is a check or restraint on those who live under the law of liberty, for *All things are lawful ... but all things are not expedient ... but all things do not edify* (1 Corinthians 10:23). We are free in all things except when the Holy Spirit indicates something different.

> 2 *If any man offends not in word, the same is a perfect man, and able also to govern the whole body with restraint.*
>
> 3 *Behold, we put bits (or restraint) in the horses' mouths to persuade them, and we govern their whole body* (James 3:2-3).

For this reason the Word says: *Walk in the Spirit, and ye shall not fulfill the lust of the flesh* (Galatians 5:16). For those who dwell in the Tabernacle of David, the check or restraint is not the clergical ministry or Levitical priesthood as in the Tabernacle of Moses under the law of death. The restraint is the Spirit of life under the law of liberty, ministrated by the priesthood of Melchizedek. The covering of those in the Tabernacle of David is the Holy Spirit.

As with the meek horse who obeys his master even without the reins and the bit, we can sense the sorrow or joy of the Spirit of God in regard to whatever we are doing. God leaves us in liberty to follow Him, but He reserves the right to pick up the reins at any given moment. For this reason we need to speak and act *as they that shall be judged by the law of liberty.*

We will be judged according to our response to the guidance of the Spirit of God in our life in regard to the unique circumstances of our situation. The Spirit may prohibit us from doing something that everyone else is permitted to do, or He may authorize and urge us to do something that seems crazy to others. But the guidance of the Spirit of God will always be in accordance with Scripture, and it will always lead us toward becoming a *perfect man that does not offend in word.*

> 1 *Now of the things which we have spoken, this is the sum: We have such a high priest who sat down at the right hand of the throne of the Majesty in the heavens,*
>
> 2 *a minister of the sanctuary and of the true tabernacle* [of David], *which the Lord pitched, and not man* [God set the ministry of Christ in the Tabernacle of David and not the ministry of man to control, order, and discipline His people] (Hebrews 8:1-2).

If David had dared to pitch this tabernacle of intimate communion with God on his own without having a clear word from God to do so, it would have cost him his life just as the new cart cost Uzzah his life. According to the revelation given by God to the prophet Isaiah, even judgment from the throne of mercy is accomplished in the Tabernacle of David.

> 5 *And in mercy shall the throne be established; and he shall sit upon it in truth in the tabernacle of David, judging and seeking judgment and hastening righteousness* (Isaiah 16:5).

For those of us who desire judgment with mercy, we can find it in the Tabernacle of David of intimate communion with God the Father through Jesus the Christ. He is willing to *judge, seek judgment, and hasten righteousness* with mercy through His Holy Spirit in those who pay the price to meet him in the Tabernacle of David.

> 5 *My son, despise not thou the chastening of the Lord, nor faint when thou art reproved of him:*

> 6 *for whom the Lord loves, he chastens, and scourges everyone whom he receives as a son.*

> 7 *If ye endure chastening, God deals with you as with sons; for what son is he whom the father does not chasten?*

> 11 *It is true that no chastening at present seems to be cause for joy, but rather for grief; nevertheless, afterward it yields the peaceable fruit of righteousness unto those who are exercised by it.*

> 12 *Therefore, lift up the hands which hang down, and the feeble knees,*

> 13 *and make straight steps unto your feet, so that which is lame will not turn out of the way* [lest that which is imperfect in your walk cause you to turn out of His way], *but let it rather be healed* (Hebrews 12:5-7, 11-13).

This healing or salvation cannot be obtained just by submission to human ministry, no matter how anointed people are, or by belonging to the ideal group. This judgment comes only to those individuals who dare to open their hearts to God in the Tabernacle of David in search of death to the ways, desires, and appetites of the old man. Then they may find their existence in Him (the new man). David found this throne of mercy. And for that reason he said:

23 *Search me, O God, and know my heart; try me, and know my thoughts*

24 *and see if there be any wicked way in me, and lead me in the way eternal* (Psalm 139:23-24).

The Tabernacle of David is the site where the materials are prepared for the edification of the true temple of God (which we are). David could not build the temple because the LORD said to him: *Thou hast shed blood abundantly and hast made great wars; thou shalt not build a house unto my name because thou hast shed much blood upon the earth in my sight* (1 Chronicles 22:8).

Nevertheless, throughout the age of the church, many individuals and groups involved in wars and with blood on their hands have not hesitated to attempt to build the temple of the Lord in the form of a given denomination, group, or organized movement. These attempts resulted in building dead monuments instead of joining living stones that would be a light unto the nations. Man measures success by the number of participants, or by the installations according the criteria of this world, while God measures success by righteousness in the heart and obedience to His Word by those who have learned His ways.

Our human efforts to build the corporate temple of God will continue to fail until we understand that first the materials (the individual stones in their natural state) must be processed in the Tabernacle of David before the throne of mercy by Him who *judges, seeks judgment, and hastens righteousness* in each individual stone. If the individual stones are not ready, it is vain to attempt to join them one to another.

Let us listen to the *Song of Degrees* or *Ascent* written for Solomon (the only one who was chosen by God to build the temple with the materials that had been prepared beforehand by his father David).

This was the song of the people of God as they came up to Jerusalem to celebrate the feasts of the Lord three times each year.

1 *Unless the LORD builds the house, they labour in vain that build it; unless the LORD keeps the city, the watchmen watch in vain* [those who build kingdoms have to watch out for them and never find rest because it is all in vain].

2 *It is vain for you to rise up early, to come home late, to eat the bread of sorrows, because he shall give his beloved sleep* [and while He gives her rest in the Tabernacle of David, in intimate communion with Himself, true spiritual offspring will be conceived and born].

3 *Behold, sons are a heritage of the LORD* [the true children of the LORD who are born by the Spirit do not belong to any human institution or ministry], *and the fruit of the womb is to be desired* [the LORD is jealous for them].

4 *As arrows in the hand of a mighty man* [in the hand of Jesus], *so are the young men* [those who are coming to maturity in Christ and overcome the evil one (1 John 2:13)].

5 *Happy is the* [mature] *man* [the mature son, Christ, the manchild who has come to the fullness of maturity or perfection] *that has filled his quiver with them* [of overcomer sons]: *he shall not be ashamed when he speaks with the enemies in the gate* [soon the corporate sons of God with Jesus as the head will speak with the enemies at the gate, and they will not be ashamed. Satan will not have a valid accusation against any in this company because they will be completely dead unto sin and alive in Christ]

(Psalm 127, translated from the 1569 old Spanish Scriptures of the Reformation).

Under the old covenant, everything that God required could be fulfilled in family except the three annual feasts of the LORD and certain sacrifices that had to be offered in Jerusalem. Over time, men added worship in the synagogues with their seats of honor and the possibility of being thrown out of the synagogue for offending the Jews who occupied these seats as a measure for intensifying human control.

The same thing happened in the Christian era as capable and organized men did not content themselves with the Tabernacle of David where each believer had sweet communion with God, and the Holy Spirit was in charge of the when and how of the meetings or assemblies and the giving out of the gifts and ministries according to the sovereign will of God.

For those corporate expressions that are ordained of God, He will set the proper governments in place to ensure that His work is accomplished, according to His due order. Under certain circumstances He will intervene directly if the authority He has delegated is despised. Those who receive authority and responsibility from God do not have to consciously defend it.

As in the case of Moses, David, Elijah, Peter, and Paul, God will justify and defend that which is an extension of Himself. Instead of defending and justifying their ministry and authority, those in God's true government will often find themselves in intercession, pleading with God to show mercy on those who have despised their authority in the Lord.

When man precipitates horizontal union outside of the timing and ways of God, leaven will be incorporated into the lump (Luke 13:21), and to maintain order, human ministry with a strong hand will be required to control the *goats* that are in the sheepfold disguised as sheep. When this happens, the ministry often ends up mistreating and hurting the true sheep, slowing their growth, and delaying their maturity. Nevertheless, the LORD promises that *unto those who love God, all things help them unto good, to those who according to the purpose are called to be saints* (Romans 8:28).

God has permitted all the human attempts and endeavors to build kingdoms in His name because He is an expert in using adversity and injustice to dress and purify the true living stones that He is planning to use in the construction of His true temple when the time comes. Men can continue with their grandiose plans and programs that are always in vain and come to nothing. And Jesus the Christ continues, seated in truth in the Tabernacle of David, preparing and purifying each individual stone, one by one, until the time comes to put together His true temple, built without hands and without the sound of a hammer.

In the Tabernacle of David, the meeting of two or three in the name of the LORD produces glorious happenings in the course of a daily walk with Jesus. Like a certain occasion on the road to Emmaus, the presence of Jesus caused the hearts of the disciples to burn within them. In the Tabernacle of David, the presence of God can be as real to a solitary prisoner in a cell or someone who has been kidnapped by guerrillas in the jungles of South America as in the assembly of hundreds or thousands of Christians.

To those who have found the great blessing of the Tabernacle of David – of intimate communion with God under the new covenant – the LORD would say:

> 16 *This is the testimony that I will make with them ... I will give my laws in their hearts, and in their souls will I write them* [the will of God will be written into their personality,

into their feelings, and into their thoughts as an integral part of their will so that they will want what He wants, and their heart's supreme desire will be to please God];

17 *and their sins and iniquities will I remember no more.*

19 *Having therefore, brethren, boldness to enter into the sanctuary* [in this tabernacle where the ark of the presence of God the Father resides] *by the blood of Jesus,*

20 *by a new and living way, which he has consecrated for us, through the veil, that is to say, his flesh;*

21 *and having that* [unique] *great priest* [of the order of Melchizedek] *over the house of God* [there is no human hierarchy; there are gifts and ministries given by Him that should produce a reflection of Him (in part) in us until that which is perfect is come (1 Corinthians 13 and Ephesians 4)],

22 *let us draw near with a true heart* [cleansed from the lies and desires of self] *in full assurance of faith* [in Him to completely change us into His image and likeness], *having our hearts purified from an evil conscience* [through the fire of His discipline and dealings] *and our bodies washed with pure water* [from hearing and obeying His living Word].

23 *let us hold fast the profession of our hope* [of having part in the first resurrection and forming part of the kingdom of God as a living stone] *without wavering (for he is faithful that promised)*

24 *And let us consider one another* [now, after being joined to Christ, comes the second phase which is to learn to consider one another] *to provoke unto charity* [the redemptive agape

love that only comes from God and is born out of sacrifice] *and unto good works* [ordered and initiated by Him and carried out by us with His resources],

25 *not forsaking our gathering together, as the manner of some is* [some Hebrews who had discovered the great revelation of the restored Tabernacle of David – of intimacy with God under the new covenant– did not bother to ever go back and exhort those among the congregation of the Jews who had never heard this revelation], *but exhorting one another and so much the more, when ye see that day approaching* [in Paul's day, judgment was rapidly approaching the Jews of natural Israel after the end of the 1500-year age of the law (Jerusalem was destroyed about AD 70), and in our day, judgment is rapidly approaching for spiritual Israel as the 2000-year age of grace is about finished, and the lukewarm church is about to go through great tribulation].

(Hebrews 10:16-17, 19-25, translated from the 1569 old Spanish Scriptures of the Reformation).

Here the Lord is telling us that the results of our permanent encounter with Him in the Tabernacle of David should be manifested in two ways:

1. On an individual level we must *draw near with a true heart in full assurance of faith, having our hearts purified from an evil conscience, and our bodies washed with pure water* [that we might be properly joined to Him].

This is necessary for us to be properly joined to the rest of the members of the body of Christ and to learn to treat others in the following manner:

2. And let us consider one another to provoke unto charity [this highest form of love only comes from God and is demonstrated in those willing to lay down their own life for their brother] *and unto good works* [that the mercy and good will of God may flow through us to others now that we are clean vessels in His hand], *not forsaking our gathering together, as the manner of some is, but exhorting one another and so much the more, when ye see that day* [of the LORD] *approaching.*

The manner of Paul, for all his life, was to not forsake the congregation of the Hebrews who did not have the revelation that he had. Even after being jailed for years as a result of the opposition of the Jews, when he arrived in Rome in chains, the first thing he did was to call a meeting of the congregation of the Jews in Rome that he might exhort them regarding the intimate relationship that is available with God through the Lord Jesus Christ (Acts 28:17-29).

What Paul meant when he wrote about *not forsaking our gathering together* (a phrase that has been mistranslated in a number of English Bibles) was that he continued to have a place in his heart for the Jews and was willing to continue to risk his own life to keep on exhorting them to receive the truth. He did not mean that we should take a willing part in dead, legalistic ritual and in the Babylonian-type human control over others that is practiced by those who do not have a revelation of the Tabernacle of David.

Sadly, the manner of some who have received the great revelation of the intimacy with God is to never return to the religious prisons (the congregations where they once gathered before receiving greater light from God) to exhort those that they left behind. They abandon those who might also be converted to the truth and escape the great tribulation of the day of the LORD that is about to descend upon most of the church.

Others twist this verse to require the people to attend their endless man-ordained meetings. At the end of the book of Acts, on the third day after Paul arrived in Rome – in chains – in the midst of a number of trials and tribulations, he congregated the Jews *(not forsaking our gathering together, as the manner of some is)* for the purpose of exhorting them.

> 23 *And when they had appointed him a day, many came to him into his lodging* [because Paul was a prisoner and could not go to the synagogue], *to whom he expounded and testified the kingdom of God, procuring to persuade them of that concerning Jesus, the Christ, out of the law of Moses and out of the prophets, from morning until evening.*
>
> 24 *And some believed the things that were spoken, and some did not believe* (Acts 28:23-24).

This gospel of the kingdom will be preached in the entire religious world, as well as to those who are worldly, before the end shall come. As was the manner of Paul on all of his missionary journeys to preach first to the Jew and then to the Gentile, even though he was the apostle to the Gentiles, so shall the overcoming sons of God do who will live and preach *this gospel of the kingdom ... in all the world for a witness unto all nations, and then shall the end come* (Matthew 24:14) They will begin by proclaiming this message in the lukewarm churches, causing these people to choose between being cold or hot or being spewed out of God's mouth. As cleansing and judgment progress in the house of God, there will be a clearer and sharper message for those who are worldly and for those who are apostate before the end comes because:

8 *Behold, the eyes of the LORD GOD are against the sinful kingdom, and* [it does not matter how pious and wonderful this kingdom appears to the natural eye if it does not produce good fruit in the allotted season] *I will destroy it from off the face of the earth saving that I will not utterly destroy the house of Jacob* [I will leave those who truly desire to attain to my real kingdom, even if they have made some mistakes at the beginning by walking according to the flesh, provided that they are willing to pay the price], *saith the LORD.*

9 *For, behold, I will command, and I will cause the house of Israel* [of all those who have agreed to die to their own way] *to be sifted among the Gentiles* [denominations of those religious Gentiles who are not circumcised in their hearts] *like as the grain is sifted in a sieve, yet shall not the least grain fall to the earth* [no matter what mistreatment they suffer at the hands of those who build religious kingdoms in my name, no one will pluck them out of my hand as I perfect them in the midst of injustice].

10 *All the sinners of my people shall die by the sword, who say, For our sake the evil shall not come near nor overtake us* [even though it is necessary that offenses and injustices come, woe to those who are the cause of it].

11 *In that day will I raise up the Tabernacle of David that is fallen and close up its breaches; and I will raise up its ruins, and I will build it as in the days of old* [as when I established the house of David forever in righteousness for the glory and praise of God in all the earth]:

12 *that those who are called by my name may possess the remnant of Edom* [the land of the doers or builders of their own kingdoms] *and all the Gentiles* [the day will come when the uncircumcised of heart will be ruled by those who are circumcised of heart; by the sons of God who have overcome], *saith the LORD that does this.*

(Amos 9:8-12, translated from the 1569 old Spanish Scriptures of the Reformation).

In our present day, many twist the concept of praise to mean that which is done in a meeting with good musicians, good voices, and a high-powered sound system, even if the lives of many of the participants are still in sin and defeat. True praise before God comes from a daily walk in victory and in holiness.

In his Psalms, David refers to the little tent pitched in his backyard where the glory of God resided as a type or shadow of something he calls the "House of the LORD" or "His Tabernacle." David knew that security and salvation are only found in Him and not in a certain geographical location. The praise of David was the product of a walk in holiness and victory before the Lord. His praise was the product of the discipline and severe dealings of God in his life, as he said that only:

4 *One thing have I desired of the LORD, that will I seek after: that I may dwell in the house of the LORD all the days of my life to behold the beauty of the LORD and to enquire in his temple* [God gave David the plans to the temple, while he *beheld the beauty of the LORD* in the Tabernacle of David, because He is the pattern, and the temple is us conformed to the image and likeness of Jesus Christ in a body of many members].

5 *For in the time of trouble he shall hide me in his tabernacle* [under His covering]; *in the secret of his tent shall he hide me; he shall set me high upon a rock* [when we are under His covering we are safe and secure regardless of the circumstances going on in the world around us].

6 *And now shall mine head be lifted up above my enemies round about me* [in David, God restored to natural Israel all that He had promised them in regard to their borders and victory over their enemies]; *therefore I will offer sacrifices of joy in his tabernacle* [this is the same word used to describe the trumpet blast that would sound every fiftieth year on the Day of Atonement to mark the beginning of the year of Jubilee (Leviticus 25:9), which is when all God's people who have sold themselves into slavery are set free, and everything is returned to the original owner]; *I will sing, yea, I will sing praises unto the LORD* (Psalm 27:4-6).

1 *The earth is the LORD'S, and the fullness thereof; the world, and they that dwell therein* [He is the original owner, and there is real jubilee or praise only as everyone and everything is returned to His authority and covering].

3 *Who shall ascend into the hill of the LORD* [into Zion where the Tabernacle of David was pitched and where the temple will be built]? *or who shall stand* [and be able to remain] *in the place of his holiness* [before the ark of the glory of His presence]?

4 [only] *He that has clean hands and a pure heart, who has not taken my name in vain* [to make or defend human

kingdoms], *nor sworn deceitfully* [when he promised to die to his own way upon being baptized into Jesus the Christ].

5 *He shall receive the blessing from the LORD, and righteousness from the God of his saving health* [Those who attempt to come into the presence of God through praise, when their hands and hearts are unclean, are guilty of taking His name in vain, and they have sworn allegiance unto Him deceitfully. They are in grave danger of coming under the curse of God if they do not repent and allow Him to cleanse them, because in their present state He will not permit them to form part of His true temple built without hands] (Psalm 24:1, 3-5, translated from the 1569 old Spanish Scriptures of the Reformation).

The Temple of God

When the time came to assemble the (corporate) temple from all the (individual) materials prepared by David according to the plans that he received from the Lord,

> *David, the king said unto all the congregation, Only Solomon, my son, has God chosen; he is young and tender, and the work is great, for the palace is not for man, but for the LORD God. Now I have prepared with all my might for the house of my God. Then the people rejoiced to have offered willingly, because with perfect heart they offered willingly to the LORD. Likewise, David the king rejoiced with great joy and blessed the LORD before all the congregation* (1 Chronicles 29:1-2, 9-10).

> *Then Solomon began to build the house of the LORD at Jerusalem in Mount Moriah* [where Isaac was offered in type and shadow of the perfect and voluntary sacrifice of Christ] *which had been shown unto David his father, in the place that David had prepared in the threshing floor of Ornan, the Jebusite* (2 Chronicles 3:1).

Here we see three important features regarding the construction of the true habitation of God (the corporate temple), which is us:

1. Only Solomon was chosen to direct this work. And for the age of the kingdom, which is at the door, God has also chosen only one man, a corporate man with Jesus as the head to direct this work.

2. The participation of those designated was completely voluntary; only for those who wished to do so willingly and with a *perfect heart* were involved. No mention was made of tithes or obligation. No threats were made (direct or indirect) of insecurity or calamity upon those who did not choose to participate. This (corporate) temple that will be for the habitation of God and not for man will be constituted by those who have given themselves over unto Him of their own free will, to be dressed and perfected as individual stones by His hand in the Tabernacle of David until they can come forth with a *perfect heart* to be joined to others.

3. The temple was constructed over a threshing floor (where a harvest had been threshed). At the end of the age of the church, the harvest will be threshed, and not only are the tares separated from the wheat, but the chaff must also be separated from the wheat before God will have the materials ready to commence construction. This great temple of God for a light unto the nations (which is His redeemed and victorious people) will be constructed over the threshing floor of the Feast of Tabernacles to bring the fullness of the kingdom of God in the earth.

In the present moment of perplexity and uncertainty regarding what should be our next individual or corporate step, let us be reminded that in all of the examples in Scripture, God chose His human vessels, gave them revelation with great clarity regarding what they were to do, and guided them step by step when it was His time for them to act.

Moses received clear and direct instructions starting with the revelation of the fire of God in the burning bush. Joshua had a face-to-face encounter with the captain of the hosts of the LORD in person. Elijah passed through wind and earthquake and fire to encounter the still, small voice of God that spoke to him with great clarity. Elisha passed through the Jordan of actual death to sin (to the old man and all that he represents) and was separated from Elijah by a chariot of fire, while Elijah was caught up to God in a whirlwind. The heavens were opened unto Jesus in the Jordan, and He received the anointing without measure to do only the will of His Father in heaven. The apostles of the first century had a clear revelation of the fire of the glory of God. All of them, including Paul, received their commission directly from Him, face to face seeing His glory.

And He promises that *the glory of this latter house shall be greater than of the former.* The new wine shall be more excellent than the old. The work that He will accomplish at the end of the age will be more glorious than what He did in the first-century church!

Let us be patient brethren and wait for the LORD. It is sad and hopeless to begin an apostolic work of joining stones in the construction of His temple without having a sharp and clear revelation of the fire of the glory of God and of His perfect will regarding the matter. Let us desist from doing work in His name that will have to be dismantled or that will be consumed in the fire of the great and terrible day of the Lord that is even now at the door.

If we are uneasy or uncertain regarding our role in the unfolding plans and purposes of God, let it be enough for us, as it was for King David in the days of old, to seek rest in the Tabernacle of David that we might ask one thing only of the Lord:

4 *that I may dwell in the house of the LORD all the days of my life to behold the beauty of the LORD and to enquire in his temple* [to receive knowledge in the revelation of Him].

5 *For in the time of trouble he shall hide me in his tabernacle.*

14 *Wait for the LORD: be of good courage, and he shall strengthen thine heart; wait, I say, for the LORD*

(Psalm 27:4-5, 14, translated from the 1569 old Spanish Scriptures of the Reformation).

Yes, brethren, let us fix our gaze upon Him and wait for Him.

The Tabernacle of David – Russell M. Stendal
This book was originally published in Spanish and English in Colombia, South America, 1994.

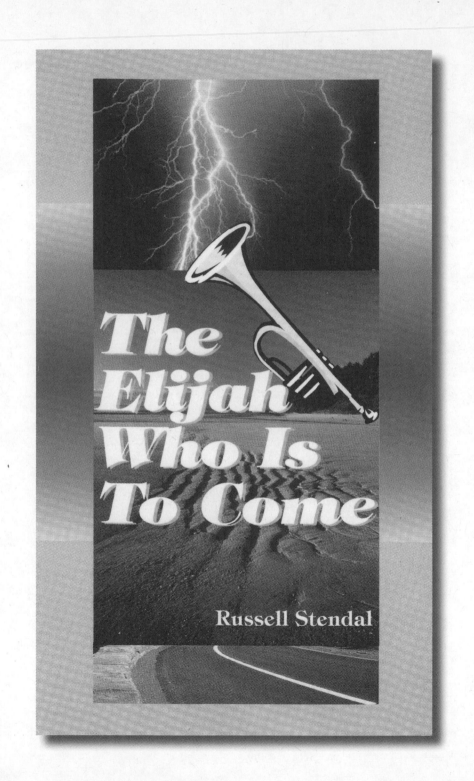

The Elijah Who Is To Come

Russell Stendal

The Elijah Who is to Come

The plan and purpose of God to restore his house.

Russell Stendal

LIFE SENTENCE
—Publishing, LLC—

Introduction

1 And I turned, and lifted up mine eyes, and looked, and, behold, there came four chariots out from between two mountains; and those mountains were of brass [symbolic of judgment].

2 In the first chariot were red horses; and in the second chariot black horses;

3 And in the third chariot white horses; and in the fourth chariot grisled and bay horses.

4 Then I answered and said unto the angel that talked with me, What is this, my lord?

5 And the angel answered and said unto me, These are the four spirits of the heavens, which go forth from standing before the Lord of all the earth (Zechariah 6:1-5).

Zechariah prophesied regarding the dealings of the Spirit of God (represented above by different colored horses in four chariots) upon a remnant that would be led out of Babylon (confusion) to restore the house of the Lord in Jerusalem. They must first pass through the two "brass" mountains of the judgments of God before they can qualify for this important work. In verse 11, Joshua (Jesus in Hebrew), the son of Josedech, the high priest, receives a crown of silver (symbolic of redemption) and gold (symbolic of the nature of God) along with the following word:

12 *And speak unto him, saying, Thus spoke the LORD of hosts, saying, Behold the man whose name is The BRANCH; and he shall grow up out of his place, and he shall build the temple of the LORD:*

13 *he shall build the temple of the LORD; and he shall bear the glory, and shall sit and rule upon his throne; and he shall be a priest upon his throne*

15 *And those that are far off shall come and build in the temple of the LORD, and ye shall know that the LORD of hosts hath sent me unto you. And this shall come to pass, if ye will obediently hear the voice of the LORD your God* (Zechariah 6:12-13, 15).

This took place in the type and shadow of the historic dealings of God with the natural Jew. It is also prophetic of what is about to happen to the spiritual Israel of God at the end of this age of the gospel being sent to the Gentiles.

In Revelation 6, we see the prophecy of the horses of Zechariah 6 amplified and clarified in yet a greater dimension regarding the plan and purpose of God to restore his house (we are the temple of God according to 1 Corinthians 3:16). This will be accomplished *not by might, nor by power*, but by the dealings of the Spirit of God in and through a prophetic company that will help to prepare the people of God for the second coming, just as John the Baptist prepared the way for the first coming of the Lord Jesus Christ (Isaiah 40:1-8).

The covenant of God (the little scroll) must be unsealed and applied to the lives of those who are called to this ministry until it becomes part of them (they must eat the scroll). When this takes place, they will not have just another message or revelation from God; they will become the message and revelation of God. As the prophet Isaiah said on a former day:

> 18 *Behold, I and the children whom the LORD hath given me are for signs and for wonders in Israel from the LORD of hosts, who dwells in mount Zion* (Isaiah 8:18).

This message will only be unsealed, revealed, and applied to those who follow the Lamb. The way of the Lamb is the way of the cross. It is the way of judgment on the old man with all his lusts and appetites until we are fully formed as the new man in Christ that *hungers and thirsts after righteousness.*

> 1 *And I saw when the Lamb had opened the first seal, and I heard the first of the four animals, saying as with a voice of thunder, Come and see.*
>
> 2 *And I saw, and behold a white horse: and he that sat upon him had a bow; and a crown was given unto him: and he went forth victorious, that he might also overcome .*

The first thing that the Lord wants to conquer is us. Will we let him shoot the arrows of His truth into all the hidden recesses of our being until we are white and pure? Judgment with mercy is available for those who submit to the dealings of God now.

> 3 *And when he had opened the second seal, I heard the second animal, which said, Come and see.*
>
> 4 *And another horse went forth that was red: and unto him that was seated thereon was given power to take away the peace of the earth, and that they should kill one another: and there was given unto him a great sword* (Revelation 6:1-4).

The sword of the truth cuts *to the dividing asunder of soul and spirit.* Jesus said (regarding His first coming) that He didn't come to bring peace, but a sword. When we enter into covenant with God on His terms, things will get worse instead of better for our natural man. The Spirit of God will begin to slice and cut away our old appetites, plans, ambitions, feelings, and desires.

When the red blood of Jesus is applied to us, His death becomes our death, just as His life now becomes our life. The two-fold purpose of the ministry of the Spirit of God becomes clearer. On the one hand, He is out to tear down and destroy the old man that we inherited from our ancestor, Adam. On the other hand, His purpose is to bless and prosper us as the new man in Christ until we come to maturity (perfection).

> 5 *And when he had opened the third seal, I heard the third animal, which said, Come and see. And I saw, and behold a black horse; and he that was seated upon him had a yoke in his hand.*
>
> 6 *And I heard a voice in the midst of the four animals, which said, A choenix of wheat for a denarius, and three choenix of barley for a denarius; and see thou hurt not the oil and the wine* (Revelation 6:5-6).

The ways of the LORD seem very black to our natural way of thinking. His thoughts are not our thoughts; His ways are not our ways. Yet, he *supplies all our need according to His riches in glory.* He starts by giving us our daily bread; a *measure of wheat for a penny.* He is the wheat (for *man doth not live by bread only, but by every word that proceedeth from the mouth of the LORD*). A penny, or denarius, was a day's wage.

God expects us to put in a full day with Him from dawn to dusk. We are to depend on His every word that we might learn to *walk in the Spirit and not fulfill the lust of the flesh.* This is the walking out in actual practice of the redemption that Jesus provides for us at our spiritual Passover (the natural feast was celebrated at the time of the winter wheat harvest).

If we are faithful with little, we will be given more. We will be given *three measures of barley for a penny.* We will be given gifts and blessings so we might, in turn, bless others. We are still expected to *work* [or walk] *out our salvation with fear and trembling* and earn our "penny" by putting in a full day with the Lord. But we are to learn to rest from our own works that we might walk in His works, the works of faith (James 2:20-26). The barley harvest was at the time of the feast of Pentecost.

The blessings and gifts of our personal Pentecost (typed/symbolized by the number 3) go well above and beyond what is necessary to meet our own needs. The baptism of the Spirit of Pentecost (the down payment on our inheritance in Christ) is for the purpose of bringing us into ministry (service) unto others.

As we walk with God through the personal appropriation of Passover and Pentecost, we begin to look forward with great expectations to the Feast of Tabernacles – Tabernacles, the feast of fullness, the feast of the entire harvest. If we are told to expect one measure of wheat at Passover and three measures of barley at Pentecost, what might we expect at the Feast of Tabernacles? Seven measures of oil and wine? Ten measures? Twelve measures?

Instead we are issued a solemn warning: *see thou hurt not the oil and the wine*! The oil of the anointing and the wine of the new life in Christ can be "hurt" if we are not careful with our blessing of Pentecost. Our spiritual gifts and blessings can be placed on the altar and used to foment the kingdom of God if we continue to *seek first the Kingdom of God and His righteousness,* or they may be used for personal gain.

Those who opt for personal gain and use the blessing and provision of God to attempt to satisfy their insatiable carnal appetites will be allowed to have their *pot of porridge* now at the expense of their *birthright* later. Those who operate in ministry and/or in spiritual gifts for personal gain will sooner or later hurt the oil and the wine. This vast discrepancy between their walk and their talk will catch up with them.

> 7 *And when he had opened the fourth seal, I heard the voice of the fourth animal, which said, Come and see.*
>
> 8 *And I looked, and behold a green horse: and he that was seated upon him was named Death, and Hades* [grave] *followed with him. And power was given unto him over the fourth part of the earth, to kill with sword, and with hunger, and with death, and with the beasts of the earth* (Revelation 6:7-8).

God repented that He ever made the natural man and vowed to destroy him (Genesis 6:1-7). God is not out to rehabilitate our old self with its old carnal appetites and desires; He is out to destroy it. He will not rest until it is dead, buried with Christ. *Therefore if anyone is in Christ, they are a new creation: old things are passed away; behold, all things are made new* (2 Corinthians 5:17). Many of us believe this in theory, but God wants it walked out in actual practice so that by the Spirit, we *mortify the deeds of the body.*

The green horse is given power over the fourth part of the earth (the earth or land is symbolic of the people of God). It is worth noting that the first time this fraction (one-fourth) is used in Scripture, it is in regard to the morning and evening sacrifice (Exodus 29:40) where one-fourth of a hin of oil and one-fourth of a hin of wine are to be given along with the morning and evening sacrifices. Jesus, the morning sacrifice (of the day of grace), poured out His oil and wine.

He did the will of the Father, being obedient even unto the death on the cross. Now, at the time of the evening sacrifice, God is looking for those who are willing to follow in the footsteps of their Master and pour out the oil and the wine onto the altar of His purposes, instead of using the anointing and the new life that He has given them for their own purposes.

> 9 And when he had opened the fifth seal, I saw under the altar the souls of those that had been slain because of the word of God, and for the testimony which they held:
>
> 10 And they cried with a loud voice, saying, How long, O Lord, holy and true, dost thou not judge and avenge our blood on those that dwell on the earth?
>
> 11 And white robes were given unto every one of them; and it was said unto them, that they should rest yet for a little while, until their fellow servants also and their brethren, that should be killed as they were, should be fulfilled (Revelation 6:9-11).

Those who have died to their own way are resting. They are given white robes (the original text implies a special or unique white robe for each of them). This is not just an imputed righteousness. This is not just the covering of Christ over the ugliness of our own flesh and carnality. This is actual righteousness walked out in the Spirit through the tribulations of everyday life until the carnal man within us, the old man that we inherited from Adam, is really dead. This applies to all the overcomers who have physically died and gone to be with the Lord, but at the time of the end, there is reference also in Scripture to those who are *alive and remain* yet have died to their own way and desires.

12 *And I saw when he had opened the sixth seal, and, behold, there was a great earthquake* [a shake-up or awakening among the people of God]; *and the sun became black as sackcloth of hair, and the moon became as blood;*

13 *And the stars of heaven fell unto the earth, even as a fig tree casts her figs, when she is shaken of a mighty wind.*

14 *And the heaven departed as a scroll when it is rolled together; and every mountain and island were moved out of their places.*

15 *And the kings of the earth, and the princes, and the rich, and the captains, and the strong, and every servant, and every free man, hid themselves in the caves and among the rocks of the mountains;*

16 *And said to the mountains and to the rocks, Fall on us, and hide us from the face of him that is seated upon the throne, and from the wrath of the Lamb:*

17 *For the great day of his wrath is come; and who shall be able to stand before him?* (Revelation 6:12-17).

For those who have died to the old carnal man and have come to maturity in the new man, *the sun shall become black as sackcloth*: the things of this world shall lose their brilliance and attraction. They shall see the *moon* [the church] *as blood.* The church under the rule of the natural man (as typified by King Saul in Israel) is a bloody mess of infighting and bickering, opening the door even unto witchcraft. God's overcomers long for a new moon that will wane no more, a moon that will shine as the sun (Isaiah 30:26). The *stars shall fall* as untimely figs. Those who shine now based on gifting without the corresponding virtue and maturity in their being shall fall on this day (the day of the Lord). This also applies to *principalities and powers in heavenly places.* For the accuser of our brethren shall be cast down when there is a people upon the earth who have died in actual practice to their own ways and desires.

The heavens shall depart as a scroll before such a people in the same manner that the heavens were opened unto Jesus when He came up out of His baptism in the Jordan River. The hitherto unfulfilled promise of God that *whatsoever ye shall ask in my name, that will I do* shall become a reality because this is a people that will not ask amiss (John 14:13, 16:26).

And the fear of the Lord shall descend once again upon the men of the earth (church). The *kings of the earth, and the great men, and the rich men, and the captains, and the strong men, and every servant, and every free man* shall suddenly realize that they have been taking the name of the Lord in vain when they have used the blessing, provision, anointing, and gifting of God for their own purposes.

> 1 *And when he had opened the seventh seal, there was silence in heaven about the space of half an hour.*
>
> 2 *And I saw the seven angels which stood before God, and to them were given seven trumpets* (Revelation 8:1-2).

When there is silence in heaven before the throne, then shall the trumpets of the message of God unfold on the Feast of Trumpets at the beginning of the great and terrible day of the Lord. A clear message through clean vessels will prevail. This is the ministry of *The Elijah That Is To Come.*

> *For the testimony of Jesus is the spirit of prophecy* (Revelation 19:10).
>
> *And Jesus answered and said unto them, Elijah truly shall first come and restore all things* (Matthew 17:11).

4 *Remember ye the law of Moses my servant, which I commanded unto him in Horeb statutes and my rights over all Israel.*

5 *Behold, I will send you Elijah the prophet before the coming of the great and terrible day of the LORD* (Malachi 4:4-5).

The promise that follows in Malachi 4:6 regarding the coming of Elijah the prophet is conditional on the above Scripture which commands us to remember our covenant with God, known as the Old or the New Testament. Both have two key stipulations that must be complied with: (1) my rights... over all Israel – God's people belong to Him and – *we are not our own, we are bought with a great price* – He is sovereign lord and master, and (2) my... ordinances over all Israel – if we are in covenant with God and belong to Him, there is a new way of doing things – His way – or His divine order. The Old Testament was written on tablets of stone, and Israel could not keep this covenant in their own strength. Under the New Testament, the resources of the Holy Spirit and fire are available to write the will of God on the tablets of our hearts, so we might keep this covenant in the power of God.

5 *Behold, I will send you Elijah the prophet before the coming of the great and terrible day of the LORD:*

6 *And he shall convert the heart of the fathers to the sons* [so that the fathers will not continue enslaving the sons in their own kingdoms], *and the heart of the sons to the fathers* [so that the sons will listen to and honor the true fathers in the Lord], *lest I come and smite the earth with destruction* [as happened to natural Jerusalem in AD 70, and as could happen to the lukewarm church of the twentieth century if we do not keep our covenant with God] (Malachi 4:4-6 translated from the old Spanish Scriptures of the Reformation, 1569).

The Restoration
of All Things

16 *And many of the sons of Israel shall he convert to the*
Lord their God.

17 *And he* [John] *shall go before him* [Jesus] *with the spirit*
and virtue of Elijah, to convert the hearts of the fathers
to the sons, and the disobedient to the wisdom of the just;
to make ready a PREPARED people for the Lord (Luke
1:16-17 translated from the old Spanish Scriptures of the
Reformation, 1569, emphasis mine).

When there is a PREPARED people in the earth, *a glorious*
church, not having spot, or wrinkle, or any such thing; but that
she should be holy and without blemish (Ephesians 5:27), we will be
able to say that the ministry of Elijah to restore *all* things has been
accomplished. While that is still not the case, we are running the
grave risk that the coming of the Lord will bring the destruction of
our land, of our lukewarm church of modern-day Laodiceans. And the
fullness of the ministry of Elijah (of God Himself in a corporate body
of overcomers) is promised by God at the same time that He reminds
us of our part in the covenant that we have with Him so we might:

(1) Always remember His rights over all Israel, giving Him
His lordship in everything.

(2) Learn to do everything His way according to His divine order.

Even after many extraordinary individual ministries, the restoration of *all* things to make ready a prepared people for the Lord has not occurred in fullness. For this reason, the Lord is preparing a corporate prophet to close the church age and to prepare the way for the second coming in a pure and perfect ministry of overcomer sons who will preach and live the fullness of *this gospel of the kingdom... in all the world for a witness unto all nations; and then the end shall come.*

Elijah means "God Himself" in Hebrew or "The Lord is God." The complete fulfillment of the ministry of Elijah is as a corporate prophet of many overcomer sons in all the fullness of God, preparing the way for the complete fulfillment of the following Scripture that has only been partially fulfilled:

67 *And his father Zacharias was filled with the Holy Spirit, and prophesied, saying,*

68 *blessed be the Lord God of Israel; for he has visited and made redemption for his people,*

69 *and has raised up a horn of saving health for us in the house of his servant David;*

70 *as he spoke by the mouth of the saints who from the beginning were his prophets* [the most important qualification to be a prophet is to be holy or clean]:

71 *salvation from our enemies, and from the hand of ALL that hate us;*

72 *to fulfill mercy unto our fathers, and remembering his holy covenant;*

73 *of the oath which he made to our father Abraham,*

74 *that he would grant unto us, that without fear delivered out of the hand of our enemies, we might serve him,*

75 *in holiness and righteousness before him, all the days of our life.*

76 *And thou, child, shalt be called prophet of the Most High: for thou shalt go before the face of the Lord to prepare his ways* [that the people might learn to do things God's way];

77 *giving knowledge of saving health unto his people for the remission of their sins* [the assurance of salvation is the victory over all known sin],

78 *through the bowels of mercy of our God; whereby the dayspring from on high has visited us,*

79 *to give light to those that dwell in darkness and in the shadow of death, to direct our feet into the way of peace.*

80 *And the child grew, and was comforted* [strengthened] *of the Spirit, and was in the deserts until the day of his showing unto Israel* (Luke 1:67-80 translated from the old Spanish Scriptures of the Reformation, 1569, emphasis mine).

In this passage, it is difficult to draw the line between where the ministry of John ends and the ministry of Jesus begins because John had – in measure – the same Spirit that descended on Jesus – without measure – (John 3:34). He was filled with the Spirit from his mother's womb when Mary visited Elizabeth (Luke 1:15, 41). But this passage will have its complete fulfillment now at the end of the church age and the beginning of the kingdom age where *we being delivered out of the hand of our enemies might serve him without fear, in holiness and righteousness all the days of our life.* And the overcomers of the last days who participate in the corporate Elijah ministry unto the *restoration of all things* will say along with the angel of Revelation 19 to those who, like the apostle John, have the temptation to worship the messenger instead of God alone: *SEE THAT THOU DO IT NOT: I am thy fellow servant, and with thy brethren that have the testimony of Jesus: worship God: FOR THE TESTIMONY OF JESUS IS THE SPIRIT OF PROPHECY* (Revelation 19:10, emphasis mine).

God promised to send the prophet to the nation of Israel because they did not want to pay the price to personally hear the voice of God. *And they said unto Moses, Speak thou with us, and we will hear: but let not God speak with us, lest we die* (Exodus 20:19). The ministry of the prophet was to Israel – to speak on behalf of God to those who did not want to pay the price. Today there are many similar situations regarding those who refuse to put off the old man, those who refuse to die to sin in all of its forms and guises.

> 15 *The LORD thy God will raise up unto thee a Prophet from the midst of thee, of thy brethren, like unto me; unto him ye shall hearken;* [Jesus is that Prophet (Acts 3:20-22)];
>
> 16 *according to all that thou didst desire of the LORD thy God in Horeb in the day of the assembly, saying, Let me not hear again the voice of the LORD my God, neither let me see this great fire any more, that I die not.*
>
> 17 *And the LORD said unto me, They have well spoken that which they have spoken* [God will not force us to pay the price of death to our own ways if we prefer to live under a covenant of law instead of grace, but for those who have not agreed to pay the price, He promises that]:

18 *I will raise them up a Prophet from among their brethren, like unto thee, and will put my words in his mouth; and he shall speak unto them all that I shall command him.*

19 *And it shall come to pass, that whoever will not hearken unto my words which he shall speak in my name, I will require it of him.*

20 *But the prophet, which shall presume to speak a word in my name, which I have not commanded him to speak... even that prophet shall die* (Deuteronomy 18:15-20).

And Moses, of whom the LORD said *and there arose not a prophet since in Israel like unto Moses, whom the LORD knew face to face,* died in the wilderness without entering the Promised Land because of one single error in his prophetic ministry due to the rebellious people. Moses said that:

21 *the LORD was angry with me for your sakes* [and it is often because of the people that the Lord has had to take home other extraordinary prophets], *and swore that I should not go over Jordan* [with my own life], *and that I should not go in* [in my own life] *unto that good land, which the LORD thy God gives thee for an inheritance:*

22 *Therefore, I must die* [to my ego, pride, and presumption] *in this land and will not pass the Jordan: but ye shall go pass* [if you fulfill your covenant with God], *and inherit that good land.*

23 *Keep yourselves, do not forget the covenant of the LORD your God, which he established with you* [the covenant of (1) the rights of God over all Israel – to give him his lordship in everything, because he bought us, and (2) His ordinances

– doing everything His way, according to divine order]
(Deuteronomy 4:21-23).

Nevertheless, after Moses' death, the devil lost the battle for his body (Jude 1:9) because Moses was *caught up to God and to his throne* and seen in the Promised Land on the Mount of Transfiguration together with Elijah (who had also been caught up to God and to His throne) in the presence of Jesus. The fulfillment of all prophetic ministry is to give the glory to God. For this reason, when Peter wanted to make three tabernacles; one for Moses, one for Elijah, and one for Jesus, there was an unforgettable voice that said, *THIS IS MY BELOVED SON, IN WHOM I AM WELL PLEASED; HEAR YE HIM... and when they had lifted their eyes, they saw no man, save Jesus only.* The Lord Jesus Christ is the complete fulfillment of all prophetic ministry.

18 *But God has thus fulfilled those things which he had showed in advance by the mouth of ALL his prophets, that his Christ should suffer.*

19 *Repent ye therefore and be converted that your sins may be blotted out, for the times of refreshing of the presence of the Lord are come;*

20 *who has sent Jesus Christ, who before was preached unto you,*

21 *whom it is certainly necessary that the heaven must receive until the times of RESTITUTION OF ALL THINGS,* [Matthew 17:11; Luke 1:16-17] *which God has spoken by the mouth of all his holy prophets since the age began.*

22 *For Moses truly said unto the fathers, A prophet shall the Lord your God raise up unto you* [Jesus Christ at the head

of a body] *of your brethren* [who are overcomers], *like unto me* [Moses did overcome in the power of God]; *him* [Jesus the Christ] *shall ye hear in all things doing whatever he shall say unto you.*

23 *And it shall come to pass, that every soul, which will not hear that prophet* [of many members who have died to their own ways that they might come under the headship of Jesus], *shall be destroyed from among the people* (Acts 3:18-23, emphasis mine).

God tells us that there will be a time when *prophecies shall come to an end, tongues shall cease, and knowledge shall come to an end. For we know in part, and we prophesy in part, But when that which is perfect is come, then that which is in part shall be done away* (1 Corinthians 13:8-10).

This is why the Scripture says: *Today if you hear his voice, harden not your hearts...* (Hebrews 3). For those who are unwilling to pay the price to hear his voice today, there is no guarantee that they will have the opportunity to do so tomorrow.

As long as the *today* mentioned by the apostle exists, there will be prophetic ministry on behalf of God to speak to those who are rebellious. The last great prophetic ministry of the church age is described in Revelation 11.

There is a difference between a gift of prophecy given to the individual versus the ministry of the prophet given to the church. God can speak through anyone He chooses whenever He desires to do so as He pours out His Spirit on all flesh. But the ministry of the prophet, the ministry of measuring the temple of that which has been built in the name of the Lord against His absolute standard of righteousness, is reserved for those who, like the apostle John, have had a direct encounter with the glory of God. They have fallen at His feet as though dead, all of their own desires and ambitions being consumed as they behold His glory. They have been placed in the ministry by the Lord Jesus Himself, and His rod has been placed in their hand.

1 *And there was given me a reed like unto a rod* [the measurement is the righteousness of God]: *and the angel stood, saying, Rise, and measure the temple of God* [we are the temple], *and the altar* [the gospel that is being proclaimed], *and them that worship therein* [to see if they measure up to the righteousness of God].

2 *But the court that is within the temple leave out* [the holy place where those who would operate the gifts of the Holy Spirit according to the whims of their own self have raised up an abomination], *and measure it not; for it is given unto the Gentiles* [the uncircumcised of heart]: *and the holy city shall they tread under foot forty and two months.*

3 *And I will give power unto my two witnesses, and they shall PROPHESY a thousand two hundred and threescore days, clothed in sackcloth* [in repentance and in intercession for their brethren who are in error].

4 *These are the two olive trees, and the two candlesticks* [the true body of Christ, the anointed one who is the light of the world; the number two would speak to us of a body with many members] *standing before the God of the earth.*

5 *And if any man will attempt to stop them, FIRE proceedeth from their mouth, and devoureth their enemies: and if any man will attempt to hurt them, he must in this manner be killed.*

6 *These have power to shut heaven, that it rain not in the days of their prophecy* [they have power to cause a famine for hearing the word of the Lord (Amos 8:11)]: *and have power over the waters* [of the river of humanism] *to turn them to blood, and to smite the* [religious kingdoms of this] *earth with all the plagues, as often as they will.*

7 *And when they shall have finished their testimony* [realizing like John the Baptist and like Moses that *He must increase, but I must decrease*], *the beast that ascendeth out of the bottomless pit shall make war against them, and shall overcome them, and kill them...*

11 *And after three days and a half the Spirit of life from God entered into them, and they stood upon their feet* [in resurrection (1 Corinthians 15:51)]; *and great fear fell upon them which saw them.*

12 *And they heard a great voice from heaven saying unto them, Come up hither. And they ascended up to heaven in a cloud; and their enemies beheld them* [they were *caught up to God and to his throne* or authority (Revelation. 12:5)].

13 *And the same hour was there a great earthquake* [a great shaking of the religious world], *and the tenth part of the city* [of religion] *fell* [into the hands of God because the tithe of all that is done in God's name belongs to Him according to law, even when those who use His name refuse to submit to His perfect will], *and in the earthquake were slain the* [personal] *names of seven thousand men* [of those who did not bow their knee to Baal (to the worship of man, including the worship of self)]: *and the remnant were affrighted* [they

quit their rebellion out of fear], *and gave glory to the God of heaven...*

15 *And the seventh angel sounded the trumpet; and there were great voices in heaven, saying, The kingdoms of this world are reduced to our Lord and to his* [corporate body of] *Christ* [of many members]; *and he shall reign forever and ever...* (Revelation 11:1-7, 11-13, 15, translated from the old Spanish Scriptures of the Reformation, 1569, emphasis mine).

With the ministry of the two witnesses, God separates the precious from the vile in the Christian world. This ministry placed by God *over the Gentiles and over the kingdoms to root out, and to destroy, and to throw down, and to cast down* (Jeremiah 1:10a) has two aspects:

(1) To free the true believers from the control of and from the cages of the modern pharaohs who have enslaved the true people of God (Exodus chapters 4-12.) They will have full authority from God similar to when Moses had to root out, pull down, destroy, and throw down every structure or ministry that has used the name of God to enslave the true believers.

And the LORD said unto Moses, See, I have raised thee up as God of Pharaoh: and Aaron thy brother shall be thy prophet Exodus 7:1, translated from the old Spanish Scriptures of the Reformation, 1569).

(2) Confrontation with the false prophets: to root out, destroy, throw down, and cast down every false religious spirit operating in the camp of God until the fire of God is restored on His altar, consuming all the wood, hay, and stubble that has been built in His name, leaving only that which is gold, silver, and precious stones (1 Corinthians 3:13).

The prophetic ministry of the two witnesses, ending in the first resurrection (Revelation 11:11-12; 1 Corinthians 15:51-52; Revelation 20:4-6), opens the door for the man child of Revelation 12. [In the original language the word translated man child in English simply means someone who is born free instead of into slavery (which is what happened to the human race). The only man since Adam born free is Jesus. And God wants us to be part of the body of Christ because *where the Spirit of the Lord is there is liberty.*] This is the enlargement of the corporate man (of which the Lord Jesus is the head), composed of all the overcomers in God of all time. This corporate man, resurrected and transformed, will be conforming the ministry of the seventh angel to manifest the kingdom of God on the earth.

The scope of this ministry includes the feeding of the woman in the wilderness, the judgment of Babylon the Great (the apostate church), the judgment of the nations, and the restoration of all creation (Revelation 11:18; 20:4). This ministry is a perfect apostolic ministry of the sons of God *to build, and to plant* (Jeremiah 1:10b) the kingdom.

It would appear that we are dealing with two back-to-back periods of time. The first period ends with the prophetic ministry of the two witnesses during the last three and one half years of the church age, separating the precious from the vile (Revelation chapter 11). The second is the apostolic ministry of the resurrected overcomers of all time to bring in the fullness of the kingdom (Revelation chapter 12) and initiate the one-thousand-year reign of the overcomer sons of God on the earth (Revelation 20:1-5). In reality, this is an enlargement and expansion of the church age (which has still not been corporately established) according to the perfect will of the Lord.

When we are come to the end of the two-thousand-year age of grace (which I believe may overlap into the seventh prophetic day), when we come to the end of two prophetic thousand-year days (and a good case can be made for this to take place in as many as twelve years past AD 2,000, as well as for several other dates), when the veil is removed between the Holy Place and the Holy of Holies in the restored temple of God in the earth (which is His body), the following Scripture will be fulfilled:

> 1 *Come, and let us return unto the LORD: for he hath torn, and he will heal us; he has smitten* [the old man], *and he will bind us up.*
>
> 2 *After two* [thousand-year] *days* [2 Peter 3:8] *he shall give us life: in the third day* [in the day of the Lord] *he will resurrect us* [the new man in Christ], *and we shall live in his sight...*
>
> 5 *Therefore I have hewed them by the prophets; I have slain them by the words of my mouth: and thy righteousness be as the light that goes forth* [as the new day dawns]
> (Hosea 6:1-2, 5).

Let us look at the ministry of the two witnesses from the angle of the ministry of the Elijah who is to come and *restore ALL THINGS*. First Kings 18:30-48 speaks of the same ministry as Revelation 11:1-13 in relation to the second of the two aspects of the ministry placed by God over the nations noted, number 2 above, to restore the true fire of God. After three and one half years of total famine in the land and after confronting the people and the prophets of Baal,

> 30 *Then Elijah said unto all the people, Come near unto me. And all the people came near unto him. And he repaired the altar of the LORD that was broken down* [and it is broken down today by those who preach that there is no need to die to our old carnal ways and live only unto God].

31 *And Elijah took twelve stones* [the number of divine order], *according to the number of the tribes of the sons of Jacob* [the supplanter that we all are when we attempt to gain the kingdom by our own means], *unto whom the word of the LORD came, saying, Israel shall be thy name* [Israel is a converted Jacob, after the dealings and confrontation with God that cripple our ability to walk on our own as with Jacob's *sinew that shrank*]:

32 *and with the stones he built an altar in the name of the LORD: and he made a trench round about the altar, as great as would contain two measures of seed* (1 Kings 18:30-32, emphasis mine).

Jesus was the grain of wheat that died to produce a harvest of *first fruits* in us. He was the perfect sacrifice of God in the morning of the era of the church almost two thousand years ago. But now has come the moment for the evening sacrifice, and there is a trench about the altar as great as would contain two measures of seed where we can take up our cross and follow Him.

Two thousand years ago Jesus fulfilled John 3:16, and now He is looking for a group of overcomers who will be the fulfillment of 1 John 3:16. He wants those who are willing to lay down their lives if necessary to rescue their brothers who are trapped in religious prisons and enslaved by religious spirits manifesting themselves through false prophets. These well-intentioned brethren have been deceived by the motives of their own hearts. *Hereby perceive we the love of God, because as he laid down his life for us: and we ought to lay down our lives for the brethren.*

33 *And he put the wood in order* [the dead and dry works that we have done in His name without being in union with

Him must be laid on the altar], *and cut the bullock* [all that is carnal including plans, feelings, desires, and even our "good" human ideas], *in pieces, and laid him on the wood, and said, Fill four pitchers with water, and pour it on the burnt sacrifice, and on the wood.*

34 *And he said, Do it the second time. And they did it the second time. And he said, Do it the third time. And they did it the third time* [we must be completely cleansed and saturated by the Word of God until we become a perfect sacrifice unto the Lord].

35 *And the water ran round about the altar; and he filled the trench also with water* [This eliminates the possibility of false or strange fire if we are completely surrendered before the true altar of God and saturated with His Word (living and written); this closes the door to deception.]
(1 Kings18:33-35).

This *trench as great as would contain two measures of seed* is the place and provision of God for those who are willing – among the mature sons of God – to *lay down their lives for the brethren.* They are willing to lay down even their "grain of wheat" that has come to maturity in the likeness of Christ at the time of the "evening sacrifice" and are willing even to lay down the God-given life, gifts, abilities, and ministries that have come to maturity and fruition within them.

At a previous date, they had identified in the death and resurrection of Jesus Christ (who was the morning sacrifice), reckoning the old man dead and partaking of the resurrection life of the new man in Christ. But now comes the actual death of that which seems good to man, a willingness to lay down our own life in obedience to the Lord for the sake of our brethren. It is the struggle (as Jesus had in Gethsemane) to be willing to lay down that which seems good and acceptable to man so that the perfect will of God might come forth in the earth.

This is the only way that corruption can put on incorruption. Jesus was the perfect grain of wheat that fell into the ground and died to produce a harvest, a firstfruits company of the same quality as the seed that was sown: a perfect bride.

But as this company has come to maturity – grain by grain throughout the church age and now at the end – it has been God's plan all along to sow the firstfruits as he did with Jesus, the first of the firstfruits. God did this that He might bring her forth in resurrection (the only way to obtain a perfect bride) and thereby reap an even greater harvest in the earth. This scene, involving great activity in the heavens as this key spiritual battle is won, is described by the prophet Hosea:

I will even betroth thee unto me in faith: and thou shalt know the LORD. And it shall come to pass in that day, I will respond, saith the LORD, I will respond to the heavens, and they shall respond to the earth; and the earth shall respond to the wheat, and the wine, and the oil; and they shall respond to Jezreel [God will sow]. *And I will sow her unto me in the earth...* (Hosea 2:20-23).

And the [true] *sons of Judah and the* [true] *sons of Israel shall be congregated together, and they shall raise up for themselves one head* [the day that God's people die to sin in actual fact and come completely under the perfect headship of the Lord Jesus Christ], *and they shall rise up from the land* [they shall overcome the world and the devil]: *for the day of Jezreel is great* [the day that God shall sow his bride in the earth] (Hosea 1:11).

36 And it came to pass at the time of the offering of the evening sacrifice, that Elijah the prophet came near, and said, LORD God of Abraham, Isaac, and of Israel [there are dozens of references in Scripture to the God of Abraham, Isaac, and Jacob, (the supplanter who tried to obtain the kingdom of God by his own means and according to his own ways), but this is one of only three times where He is called the God of Abraham, Isaac, and Israel (the God who can confront and wrestle with us all night if needs be, hoping we will let Him cripple our confidence in ourselves that He might convert us Jacobs into an Israel, a prince with God who can be sown unto perfection and multiplied in the earth)], *let it be known this day that thou art God in Israel, and that I am thy servant, and that I have done all these things at thy word* [Yes, God has a corporate prophet in this hour who can say *I have done all these things at thy word*; I have not operated on my own].

37 *Answer me, O LORD, answer me, that this people may know that thou art the LORD God, and that thou shalt convert their heart back again to thee* [this is the purpose of the ministry of Elijah (Malachi 4:6; Luke 1:16-17)].

38 *Then the fire of the LORD fell, which consumed the burnt sacrifice* [the tendencies to operate in the flesh], *and the wood* [the dead works], *and the stones* [the divine order of an era that has served its purpose and is over], *and the dust* [our Adamic nature of flesh and blood when we are transformed in the first resurrection], *and licked up the water* [the ministry that is, in part, of prophecies and tongues and ministries that will be done away when that which is perfect is come (see 1 Corinthians 13:8-10)] *that was in the trench* [this passage is a type and shadow of the same event described in Revelation 11:11-13].

39 *And seeing it, all the people fell on their faces* [not on their backs]: *and they said, The LORD, he is the God; the LORD, he is the God.*

40 *And Elijah said unto them, Seize the prophets of Baal; let not one of them escape. And they seized them: and Elijah took them down to the brook Kishon, and slew them there* [this agrees with Revelation 11:18] (1 Kings 18:36-40).

After this, in the book of First Kings, we have the promise of the seven thousand who will not bow the knee to Baal, the ministry of the double portion of Elisha, the anointing of Jehu, the defeat of Jezebel, and the spiritual restoration of Israel.

In our present day, as in the days of old, only one true prophet will face the hundreds of false prophets. This one and only true prophet is the Lord Jesus, the Christ in a corporate body of men and women who have demonstrated a willingness to die to sin. Only if we have placed all that is represented by the flesh and our own desires (even if they seem to be good) on the restored altar of God, will we be candidates for the last prophetic ministry of this age which will prepare the way for the glorious return of Jesus Christ and the fulfillment of Romans 8:19.

And the child grew, and was comforted of the spirit, and was in the deserts till the day of his showing unto Israel (Luke 1:80). This corporate John the Baptist that God is preparing for a key ministry in the last years of the era of Pentecost is not to be found in the limelight, inside the Christian camp that is organized and controlled by man. For he is *the voice of one crying in the wilderness, Prepare ye the way of the Lord...*

Therefore: 4 *Remember ye the law of Moses my servant* [the people of Israel obtained this old covenant of the letter that kills because they did not want to pay the price to continue to personally hear the voice of the Lord], *which I entrusted unto him in Horeb my rights* [He wishes to give us a new name – Thou art Mine – and to cover us with the spirit of His lordship under a new covenant of freedom in Him] *and ordinances* [there is a new manner of doing things if we are in covenant with Him – His way – according to due order] *over all Israel* [over all who bear His name].

5 *Behold, I will send you Elijah the prophet* [to give a sharp and clear message to all the "Christians" of today who have not paid the price to continue to hear the voice of the Lord for themselves so that they may enter into self-judgment while there is still mercy] *before the coming of the great* [for the overcomer sons of God] *and dreadful* [for those Christians who build kingdoms to control others according to their own ways in the name of the Lord] *day of the LORD:*

Will our generation learn this great lesson and permit the Holy Spirit to dismantle all that we have done in the name of God that was not included in His perfect plan and design? Where the fruits of repentance are manifest in the context of the covenant that we have with the Lord, giving him His rights over all Israel and to follow only His ordinances, is the hope that:

6 *And he* [God through the ministry of an Elijah company] *shall convert the heart of the fathers to* [place] *the sons* [in freedom before the guidance, dealings, and discipline of the Lord]*, and the heart of the sons to* [honor and respect] *the fathers* [in the Lord without making a personality cult around them]*, lest I come and smite the land with destruction* [being forced to destroy all the private kingdoms that have been built in My name before I can usher in My kingdom in fullness] (Malachi 4:4-6 translated from the old Spanish Scriptures of the Reformation, 1569).

Final Thoughts

The Feast of Trumpets was celebrated on the first day of the seventh month (Leviticus 23:24; Numbers 29:1). We are now about to enter the first year of the seventh millennium. The message of the Feast of Trumpets will be fulfilled spiritually in the people of God. Just as the redemption of Passover was fulfilled in the death and resurrection of Jesus, and the first fruits of Pentecost is fulfilled in the effusion of the Holy Spirit, we look forward to the fullness of our inheritance in the fulfillment of the Feast of Tabernacles.

The Feast of Tabernacles has three parts: (1) The Feast of Trumpets on the first day of the seventh month; (2) the Day of Atonement on the tenth day of the seventh month; and (3) the Feast of Tabernacles beginning the fifteenth day of the seventh month and lasts for seven days. At present, there is a little uncertainty as to exactly when all of this will take place.

> *Blow the shofar in the new moon, in the time appointed, on our solemn feast day* (Psalm 81:3).

The Jewish months began on the day of the new moon. Back then it was impossible for them to establish the exact date for the Feast of Trumpets with absolute certainty. It might be today or maybe tomorrow. The Sanhedrin had to actually see the new moon in order to authorize the trumpet to be blown. This, in turn, set in motion an absolute time-table to the Day of Atonement on the tenth day and to the beginning of the Feast of Tabernacles on the fifteenth day.

Today, we are in a similar situation regarding the beginning of the seventh millennium (which is the prophetic day of the Lord). It could begin this year, or next year. The only way to tell for sure that we have indeed entered the day of the LORD is to observe the new moon (according to the way God reckons time, it is first the *evening* and then the *morning* that make up the day). Isaiah the prophet spoke of a new thing (Isaiah 43:19; Numbers 16:30).

This is the coming together of the people of God in a different manner than we have ever seen before. This is a corporate expression of a new order, reflecting the light of the Son of God, waxing brighter and brighter until the moon shines as the sun in God's new day (Isaiah chapter 30). This is a coming together in the very nature of God (2 Peter chapter 1) instead of coming together around a message, a ministry, or a given group, be it denominated or undenominated, as we do now. This new moon will start as a tiny sliver of light in the pitch blackness of Saul's kingdom that will grow and grow as the house of David (the corporate expression of God in the new man) is strengthened and as the house of Saul (the corporate expression of the people of God under the old man, gifted as he may be) crumbles.

This new moon will become a full moon by the fifteenth day of the seventh month (symbolic of the seventh millennium) and will wane no more. On God's timetable regarding the tenth day of the seventh month, which is the Day of Atonement, all those who do not *afflict their souls* will be *cut off from among the people of God*. This is the reason for the message of the Feast of Trumpets. It is to prepare and warn the people of God that they must give up their own way; they must lay down their carnal appetites and desires; they must put every vestige of the old man on the altar so that God might corporately cleanse His people on the Day of Atonement. On the Day of Atonement, judgment will fall on any residue of the old man left among the people of God.

40 *As therefore the tares are gathered and burned in the fire; so shall it be in the end of this age.*

41 *The Son of man shall send forth his angels, and they shall gather out of his kingdom all things that offend, and those who do iniquity;*

42 *And shall cast them into a furnace of fire: there shall be wailing and gnashing of teeth.*

43 *Then shall the righteous shine forth as the sun in the kingdom of their Father. He Who hath ears to hear, let him hear* (Matthew 13:40-43).

Let us take a closer look at what will happen when God speaks through a corporate prophetic messenger on the Feast of Trumpets:

1 *And when he had opened the seventh seal, there was silence in heaven about the space of half an hour.*

2 *And I saw the seven angels which stood before God; and to them were given seven trumpets.*

3 *And another angel came and stood at the altar, having a golden censer; and there was given unto him much incense, of the prayers of all saints, that he should offer upon the golden altar which was before the throne.*

4 *And the smoke of the incense of the prayers of the saints, ascended up before God out of the angel's hand.*

5 And the angel took the censer, and filled it with fire of the altar, and cast it into the earth: and there were voices, and thunderings, and lightnings, and an earthquake.

Notice that when the accuser of our brethren has been cast down and there is silence before God, the golden altar of incense (the prayers of the saints) has been reestablished within the Holy of Holies. God can now restore His brazen altar (His covenant under His terms and conditions instead of the altar that has been defiled by man) so that He can multiply His remnant. The trumpets that follow are the product of the fire of God upon His restored heavenly altar.

6 And the seven angels who had the seven trumpets prepared themselves to sound their trumpets.

7 The first angel sounded the trumpet, and there followed hail and fire mingled with blood, and they were cast upon the land: and the third part of trees was burnt up, and all green grass was burnt up (Revelation 8:1-7).

The word that is to come forth in this hour is not a soft or easy word that falls like rain, causing every seed (good or bad) in the garden to grow like the effusion of the Spirit in the church age. This is a word that falls like *hail and fire mingled with blood*. This is a word that scorches, devastates, and kills.

The Third Part of the Church Shall Go Through the Fire

Trees are used throughout Scripture to describe the lives of men (Deuteronomy 20:19; Isaiah 61:3). One-third of the trees (symbolic of one-third of the people of God) shall go through the fire and be purged of their rebellion. The other two-thirds of the trees are not mentioned again in the book of Revelation. Here is clarification from the parallel passage in Zechariah 13:

8 *And it shall come to pass, that in all the land* [the land, or earth represents the people of God]*, said the LORD, two parts therein shall be cut off in her and shall be lost; but the third shall be left therein.*

9 *And I will put the third part into the fire, and will refine them as silver is refined, and will try them as gold is tried: He shall call on my name, and I will hear him: I will say, my people, and he shall say, The LORD is my God.*

This is the judgment that begins in the house of the Lord. God uses a small remnant of overcomers to give a strong, fiery word to the rest of His house and then to the world.

The Provision for the Carnal Man Shall Be Burnt Up

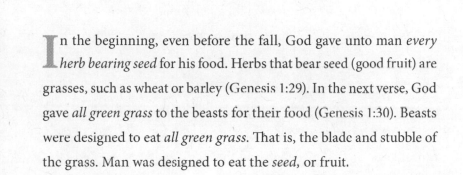

In the beginning, even before the fall, God gave unto man *every herb bearing seed* for his food. Herbs that bear seed (good fruit) are grasses, such as wheat or barley (Genesis 1:29). In the next verse, God gave *all green grass* to the beasts for their food (Genesis 1:30). Beasts were designed to eat *all green grass*. That is, the blade and stubble of the grass. Man was designed to eat the *seed*, or fruit.

Even in the natural world there are significant differences between the digestive systems of men and beasts. Man needs his grain ground up and baked into bread, while the beast can simply eat blades of grass or some hay and digest it. The grain must come to maturity in order for man to use it as food. The beast can eat grass in any stage of maturity. Only the herbs (grasses) that bear fruit (grain) can nourish man while the tares (grasses which produce the blade and the flower, but no fruit) can still nourish the beast.

It is important to note that there are exactly sixty-six verses in Scripture that mention grass or herbs. There are also sixty-six books in the Bible. There is a linkage between the concept of "grass" in the natural and the "word" in the spiritual. God said that *man doth not live by bread alone but by every word that proceedeth from the mouth of the LORD.* Jesus ties it together:

26 *He also* [Jesus] *said, So is the kingdom of God, as if a man should cast seed into the ground;*

27 *And should sleep, and rise night and day, and the seed should spring forth and grow up, he knows not how.*

28 *For the earth brings forth fruit of herself; first the blade, then the ear, after that the full grain in the ear.*

29 *But when the fruit is brought forth, immediately he puts in the sickle, because the harvest is come* (Mark 4:26-29).

Take note of the three stages of development that the seed (word) goes through after it is planted: *first the blade, then the ear* [or flower], *after that the full grain in the ear* [the mature grain or fruit]. The carnal man who is feeding his "beast appetites" with the provision of God can still feed on the "blade" and on the "ear" (or flower). He takes the blessings and provision of Passover and Pentecost and applies them to fulfilling the desires of the old man that he inherited from Adam, oblivious to the fact that this type of provision will ultimately come to an end.

5 *And the glory of the LORD shall be manifested, and all flesh shall see it together: for the mouth of the LORD has spoken it.*

6 *The voice that said, Cry. And I said, What shall I cry? All flesh is grass* [the blade], *and all the mercy thereof is as the open flower of the field* [the ear]:

7 *The grass withers, the flower fades: because the spirit of the LORD blows upon it: surely the people* [the natural man] *is grass.*

8 *The grass withereth, the open flower fades: but the word of our God* [that has come to maturity or perfection] *shall stand for ever* (Isaiah 40:5-8).

At the sound of the first trumpet of the Feast of Trumpets at the beginning of the day of the Lord, *all the green grass shall be burnt up.* This means that the provision or sustenance of the Word of God will no longer be available for those who attempt to use it for personal gain. The day of the LORD will commence with a great famine, *not a famine of bread, nor a thirst for water, but of hearing the words of the LORD* (Amos chapter 8).

The person who attempts to walk with one foot in the Spirit and the other in the flesh will get as desperate as King Ahab when he was out beating the bushes, trying to find enough grass to keep even a few horses alive (1 Kings 18:5). It will be as in the days of Joseph in Egypt. Those who do not wish to starve to death spiritually will have to surrender their walk in the flesh, because the only provision that God will have on this day is the provision to walk in the Spirit: *For if ye live after the flesh, ye shall die: but if ye through the Spirit do mortify the deeds of the body, ye shall live.*

Joseph did not store up hay and stubble for the people of Egypt to feed their beasts and then live off their herds. He stored up mature grain. When the seven years of famine hit, the first things that the people had to surrender to Joseph were their beasts, which are types and shadows of carnality and the desires of the flesh.

17 *And they brought their livestock unto Joseph: and Joseph gave them bread in exchange for horses, and for the sheep, and for the bovine livestock, and for the asses...* (Genesis 47:17).

In this example, the people had to give everything, including themselves and their lands, over to Joseph in order to remain alive.

As the trumpets of God continue to sound, this hard word, that falls like *hail and fire mingled with blood,* will devastate and destroy every natural refuge for the one-third of the "trees" that God is going to bring through the fire in such a manner as to burn up their own carnal desires and natural way of doing things. For that which is represented by this one-third, the refuge of the sea (the world) or of ships (sectarian groups), will come to an end. For this third that is being dealt with by God, the rivers and fountains of the church under man's control, will become bitter; the natural sun will become darkened (they will lose their desire for the things of this world), and so on.

Up until the end of the fourth trumpet, God appears to be dealing mainly with His people because the *judgment begins at the House of the LORD.* The next three trumpets (woes) appear to affect both the world and the people of God just as the first three plagues in Egypt affected both.

But in the fifth trumpet, the "locusts" are not allowed to touch the *green grass* of the new thing that God is doing. They can afflict only those men who do not have the seal of God on their foreheads. (They are to afflict those who don't have the mind of Christ and might interfere with the new crop that God has planted.)

In Egypt, the hail that destroyed the flax and the barley (which are types having to do with Pentecost) melted and watered the wheat and the rye! (Exodus 9:31-32). The last seven plagues in Egypt affected only that which is represented by "Egypt" and the people of God (typed by the wheat and rye) who lived in "Goshen" prospered. Fiery lightning that burns and destroys one crop also supplies essential nitrogen for the next crop.

Those who have perverted the purposes of God in Pentecost by planting an impure "barley" message and by weaving a covering of

"flax" to replace the covering of the dealings of the Holy Spirit will
be exposed and dealt with as all their work is destroyed.

14 *Therefore hear the word of the LORD, ye scornful men,
that have taken rule over this people which is in Jerusalem.*

15 *Because ye have said, We have made a covenant with
death, and with Sheol we are at agreement; when the
overflowing scourge shall pass through, it shall not come unto
us: for we have made lies our refuge, and under falsehood
have we hid ourselves.*

17 *and the hail* [of the word of the trumpets of God] *shall
sweep away the refuge of lies, and the waters shall overflow
the hiding place.*

18 *And your covenant with death shall be disannulled,
and your agreement with Sheol shall not stand; when the
overflowing scourge shall pass through, then ye shall be
trodden down by it.*

19 *From the time that it goes forth, it shall take you: for it
shall come suddenly, by day and by night: and it shall be that
the terror only causes one* [even] *to understand the report.*

20 *For the bed is shorter than that a man can stretch himself
on it: and the covering narrower than that he can wrap
himself in it.*

21 *For the LORD shall rise up as in Mount Perazim, he shall
be wroth as in the valley of Gibeon, that he may do his work,
his strange work; and bring to pass his act, his strange act*
[as when Joshua commanded the sun to stand still in type
and shadow of the day of the Lord].

22 Now therefore do not be mockers lest your bands be made strong: for I have heard from the Lord GOD of the hosts that consumption and destruction are determined upon the whole earth [church] (Isaiah 28:14-15; 17-22).

Yes, the day of man's control of the church will soon end; the day in which man has been allowed to represent God any way he pleases is almost over. From this time on, God will be represented the way He wants to be represented. He will cause Jerusalem (the people of God) to be once again a praise upon the earth. Jezebel will be overthrown once and for all and the sons of God will inherit the kingdom.

11 My days are like a shadow that declines; and I [the old man] *am withered like grass.*

12 But thou, O LORD, shalt endure for ever; and thy remembrance unto all generations.

13 Thou shalt arise, and have mercy upon Zion: for the time to favour her, the set time, is come (Psalm 102:11-13).

...And the Earth
Shall Respond
to the Wheat ...

Russell Stendal

... And the Earth
Shall Respond
to the Wheat ...

*Will you deny self and respond to the still
small voice to fulfill end-times prophecy?*

Russell Stendal

LIFE SENTENCE
──Publishing, LLC──

Praise ye the LORD for the avenging of Israel, when the people willingly offered themselves (Judges 5:2).

I am crucified with Christ; nevertheless I live; yet not I, but Christ lives in me, and the life which I now live in the flesh I live by the faith of the Son of God, who loved me and gave himself for me (Galatians 2:20).

Christ shall be magnified in my body, whether it be by life or by death. For to me to live is Christ and to die is gain (Philippians 1:20-21).

The Overcomers

2 And I saw, as it were, a sea of glass mingled with fire and those that had gotten the victory over the beast [over the *man of sin* within and without] *and over its image* [religion that ends up worshiping man along with God] *and over its mark* [man's way of thinking and acting] *and over the number of its name* [man's plans and man's ordinances or traditions implemented according to man's wisdom] *stand on the sea of glass, having the harps of God* [the true praise that comes only from walking in victory].

3 And they sing the song of Moses, the servant of God, and the song of the Lamb, saying, Great and marvellous are thy works, Lord God Almighty; just and true are thy ways, thou King of saints.

4 Who shall not fear thee, O Lord, and magnify thy name? for thou only art holy; therefore, all the Gentiles shall come and worship before thee; for thy judgments are made manifest (Revelation 15:2-4).

The overcomers, who can walk on the sea mingled with fire, are those who have been baptized with the Holy Spirit and fire. They and the sea are at rest. (The sea looks like glass.) They have been purged and disciplined and tried in the intimacy of the tabernacle of David until the old man is completely dead and the fullness of the Lord Jesus Christ is alive and has come to maturity (perfection) in them. The song of the overcomers is the song of Moses, the song of the Lamb that willingly goes to the slaughter.

The Song of Moses

Deuteronomy 32:1-43

The song of Moses has to do with the absolute righteousness, perfection, and judgment of God in relation to the continual failure of His people. When *God alone* leads His people, it results in peace and prosperity (vv. 12-14). But in prosperity God's people tend to get caught up in themselves. They begin to think that the blessing of God is a result of their own good merits and ideas, not realizing that to turn their eyes upon themselves is to forsake God and that their own righteousness *is as filthy rags* (is abominable in His sight).

This is why God complains that His people end up *provoking Him to jealousy and with abominations*. This causes God to *hide his face from them* to *see what their end shall be* (vv. 16-21). If we think we know better than God, He will let us experience the ultimate consequences of all our "good" plans and ideas. This leads to the judgment of God's people by God at the hand of their enemies (vv. 22-25). However, God wants both His people and their adversaries to know that He is the one behind these dealings (vv. 26-27). God, the writer of this song, laments:

> 29 O that they were wise, if they were prudent, they would understand their latter end!

30 *How could one chase a thousand and two put ten thousands to flight if their strong One had not sold them, and the LORD had not delivered them up?*

31 *For their strong one* [confidence in themselves in the mistaken belief that self is basically good, including confidence in the spiritual gifts and in the revelation that God has given them] *is not as our strong One* [the total confidence in God that springs from death to the old man] *and even our enemies are judges of this* [even those who do not claim to be God's people can tell the difference between the self-righteousness and spiritual pride of those who depend on the blessings and provision of God, versus the true humility and fruit of the Spirit in those who have died to their own ways, desires, and appetites and manifest the character and very life of God] (Deuteronomy 32:29-31).

The finality and severity of the judgment that begins in the house of the Lord is summed up in verses 32 through 35. Then comes a key verse with a promise:

36 *For the LORD shall judge his people and repent himself for his servants when he sees that their power is gone, and there is none shut up or left* (Deuteronomy 32:36).

When God sees that *our power is gone,* as evidenced by the fact that there is *none shut up* in the kingdoms we have built in His name *or left* under the control of others, He will *repent himself for his servants.* Our own repentance and faith can get us to the altar as far as making a covenant with God is concerned. (Our part of the covenant is to agree to die to the appetites of the flesh, the attractions of the world, and the control of the devil, placing our confidence and trust in the Lord Jesus Christ to change us into His image.

God will fulfill His part of the bargain and will share His life with us (birth us in the Spirit), give us spiritual gifts, clothe us in His righteousness, and offer to lead us with His still, small voice. But to attain to the actual righteousness and perfection (maturity) necessary to qualify us to *reign and rule with Him,* we must come to the actual death of the old man, so His life and His faith (His virtue) come forth in us.

To overcome temptations of financial and spiritual prosperity, self-righteousness, and the need to manipulate and control others, we must die to all aspects of spiritual pride. We must die even to that which we think is good in our natural selves (which Paul describes as the *old man*) if we are to completely overcome the world, the flesh, and the devil, and minister true deliverance to those around us.

The overcomers, who are the only ones who can sing the song of Moses, know that when *their power is gone* and there are *none shut up or left,* God will *repent himself for his servants.* Their power being gone means that these saints have lost the capacity to maintain or sustain a kingdom of their own. This will be demonstrated by the setting free of any who are shut up or left in any human kingdom or who are depending on or controlled by the ministry of those who have come to the place where *their power is gone.*

Anyone, still *shut up or left,* means that *their power is* [not yet] *gone.* God will not step in yet to *repent himself for his servants.* Until we completely quit trying to make God's kingdom work our own way, our group's way, or our denomination's way (according to our doctrine, "revelation" and "wisdom"), God will stand back and let everything come down around us as the time comes for our work to be *tried as by fire.*

If even the slightest dependency on our own wisdom, power, or might is left, it will leave us and possibly others *shut up or left* to our own devices. Unless these sins of commission are surrendered to the cross, we automatically prevent God from *repenting himself for us* and setting us free from the seemingly small and insignificant *sins that do so easily beset us* – the sins that time and time again deliver us back into the bondage of the enemy after we have once been delivered. As long as we think we have power in ourselves or in the gifts, revelation, anointing, and ministries that God has given us, He will step back and *hide his face* and *see what our end shall be.*

For those whose corporate or individual *power is gone,* it will be clearly demonstrated by this fact: there are *none shut up or left* captive in any type of kingdom based on right doctrine, human ministry, God-given gifts or revelations. There are *none shut up or left* who desire justification and to be proven right. There are *none shut up or left* who might cling to and rally around to denominate and make a name (individual or corporate) that is distinct from THE NAME above all names at which every knee shall bow. For those who meet this condition, God promises to *repent himself for his servants* and free them completely of all traces of sin and imperfection by the awesome power of His grace. He says to them:

> 39 ¶ *See now that I, I am he, and there are no gods with me* [there is no room for us to wield power or control what emanates from our own selves if we are to be truly joined to God]; *I kill,* [the selfish pride and arrogance of those who choose to relinquish their own power] *and I make alive* [those who are dead in Christ]; *I wound* [those who *shut up* or *leave* others in man-made kingdoms], *and I heal* [those whose power is gone]; *and there is not one that can*

deliver out of my hand [when the time is come to judge the kingdoms that have been built in my name].

40 *When I shall lift up my hand to the heavens and shall say, I live forever,* [along with those who are dead to sin and alive in me] (Deuteronomy 32:39-40).

Verses 41 to 43 speak of His judgment and vengeance on His enemies and of His mercy on His true people who have died to sin. Moses is a type and shadow of the people of God throughout the ages who learn what it is to die to their own ambitions and desires. They do this by voluntarily giving up their own power at the command of God, even when glorious deliverance, revelation, gifting, and ministry are flowing from them under tremendous anointing. These are the only ones who will sing the song of Moses, the song of the Lamb (the song of those who obey the voice of God, no matter what the consequences).

The Death of Moses

48 *And the LORD spoke unto Moses that same day, saying* [the same day Moses wrote the song of Moses],

49 *Climb up into this mountain Abarim, unto mount Nebo, which is in the land of Moab, that is over against Jericho, and behold the land of Canaan, which I give as inheritance unto the sons of Israel,*

50 *and die in the mountain which thou shalt climb and be gathered unto thy peoples* (Deuteronomy 32:48-50).

5 ¶ *So Moses, the servant of the LORD, died there in the land of Moab, according to the word of the LORD* (Deuteronomy 34:5).

Moses did not die of disease or of natural causes. He died voluntarily in obedience to the *word of the LORD*. The next two verses make this clear:

6 *And he buried him in a valley in the land of Moab, over against Bethpeor, but no one knows of his sepulchre unto this day.*

7 *And Moses was one hundred and twenty years old when he died; his eye was not dim, nor his natural force abated* (Deuteronomy 34:6-7).

Moses died in the land of Moab *according to the word of the LORD*. When the Lord told him to lay everything down, including his very life, Moses obeyed. Moses must decrease so that

Joshua (who typifies Jesus) could increase. Because of his sin of pride and arrogance (speaking his own words instead of God's words on just one solitary occasion), Moses was condemned under the law to die in the wilderness along with the rest of the people who had sinned almost continually in one way or another.

But unlike the others, Moses received very different and very special treatment. The others, even if they had the hope of future redemption by identification in the yet-future sacrifice of Jesus Christ through the blood sacrifices under the law, still went to Hades to the *bosom of Abraham* to await the climactic moment in human history when the Lord Jesus (who died as a direct result of obedience to His Father) would *descend into hell* (Hades) and *take captivity captive*. By doing that, he freed the souls of all those belonging to the Lord who had been held captive by the devil until the redemption had been paid.

Most of the rest of the men of faith of the Old Testament went to Hades, which had two compartments – one for the wicked and one for the righteous, with a great gulf between them. These righteous were awaiting redemption. Moses did not go there (Luke 16:20-31).

God, *seeing that* [Moses'] *power was* [voluntarily] *gone* decided to *repent himself for his servant* and sent Michael the archangel who *contended with the devil, disputing over the body of Moses* (Jude 9). Michael told the devil, *The Lord reprehend thee*. And the result of that encounter is evident from the accounts described in Matthew 17:3 and in Mark 9:4 where *there appeared unto them Moses and Elijah talking with him* [Jesus].

Moses and Elijah are two overcomers of the Old Testament who were not held by the power of death until the redemptive death and resurrection of the Lord Jesus Christ. They are types for the two witnesses of Revelation 11 who will also not be held by the power of death, but who will be *caught up unto God and to his throne* (Revelation 12:5) to *live and reign with Christ the thousand years* (Revelation 20:4).

The death of Moses occurred in the land of Moab. *Moab* means "the child of a woman by her own father," speaking of the incestuous child of Lot. Spiritually, Moab relates to those who attempt to be the people of God, but provide their own "father" through submission to one another, instead of submitting to God first and allowing Him to order their relationships, raising up or taking down ministries and governments as He sees fit. Moses obeyed the Lord, and God buried him such that *no one knows of his sepulchre unto this day* (Deuteronomy 34:6). This prevented a cult of worship from springing up around Moses after he was dead. Even so, there have been many attempts to deify or worship Moses.

But God had Moses die in the land of Moab and die to all that it represents. Isaiah 15 and 16 speak of the coming destruction and judgment of Moab and of the people of God who attempt to "father" themselves (in striking similarity to the judgment of the people of God in the song of Moses in Deuteronomy 32). Spiritually, Moab represents those who have the church as their "mother" but who have not or will not agree to pay the price of death to their own ways, ambitions, and desires so that they may have God as their true father. In the midst of the devastation of Moab in Isaiah 16 we find this:

> 4 *Let my outcasts dwell with thee, Moab* [let my true prophets and ministers who are *outside the camp* come in and dwell with you that they might proclaim the truth, and I might be your father once again]; *be thou a covert to them from the presence of the destroyer* [if you want to survive the judgment and devastation coming on all that Moab represents in the spiritual realm, you will need to begin to protect and

defend my true representatives]; *for the extortioner shall come to an end* [those who demand tithes and offerings to build the kingdoms of man], *the destroyer shall cease* [those who operate in the gifts and revelation of God without submitting to the Giver], *the oppressor shall be consumed out of the land* [those who choose to father themselves and who make their own kingdoms on this premise are finished; the time for this is over].

5 *And in mercy shall the throne be established; and he shall sit upon it in truth in the tabernacle of David, judging and seeking judgment and hastening righteousness.* [God is saying that, "If you will meet the conditions of verse 5, I will establish an intimate relationship with you in the tabernacle of David to father you under my direct control, discipline, and instruction until you are perfect."]

6 *We have heard of the pride of Moab* [the religious pride and arrogance of those individuals or groups that attempt to father themselves]; *he is very proud, even of his haughtiness* [an air of superiority or exclusiveness sets in] *and his pride and his wrath* [against anyone who challenges his control], *but his lies shall not be so* (Isaiah 16:4-6).

The pride, haughtiness, and arrogance of the gifted people of God are difficult to deal with. This was what caused Moses to sin (Numbers 20:7-12). The remedy occurs when we are brought completely to the end of ourselves in death, when God can see that *our power is gone*, there are *none shut up* under our control, and we are not left under someone else's control. Then God will *repent himself for his servants* and will deliver us completely from the power of sin and death as he did with Moses.

The glory would fade from Moses' face after he spoke with God in the tabernacle under the covenant of law. But the glory of God that comes from speaking with Him in the intimacy of the restored tabernacle of David under the covenant of grace is still growing. Moses was in on the ground floor of the restoration of the tabernacle of David described in Acts 15, when together with Elijah *he was talking with Jesus* in the glory of the kingdom of God of which there will be no end (Mark 9:4; Daniel 4:3; 7:18).

Elijah Seeks Death

After his great success with the restoration of God's altar and fire, culminating in the conversion of the hearts of the people back to the true God, and with the destruction of the false prophets of Baal, Elijah had a deep crisis. Even though he had been able to truthfully say *let it be known this day that thou art God in Israel and that I am thy servant and that I have done all these things at thy word* (1 Kings 18:36), Elijah came to the conclusion that he lacked something. He ran from Jezebel in an attempt to save his own life at the point that could have been a climactic moment for the spiritual restoration of Israel. The prophet began to measure his own life against the absolute standard of the righteous God and *desiring to die, he said, It is enough, now, O LORD, take away my life, for I am not better than my fathers* (1 Kings 19:4).

If we are fathered only by human teachers, we can never rise above their level. Jesus said *The disciple is not above his master, nor the servant above his lord. It is enough for the disciple that he be as his master, and the servant as his lord* (Matthew 10:24-25).

If we are to rise above the human imperfection around us and become like Jesus, we must pay the price to be fathered (taught and disciplined) by the Lord. The true bride of Christ who has been brought to perfection in the intimacy of the tabernacle of David (Acts 15; Amos 9) can claim the promise that *all thy sons shall be taught of the LORD;*

and the peace of thy sons shall be multiplied. With righteousness shalt thou be adorned (Isaiah 54:13-14).

Elijah paid the price in a forty-day death experience in the wilderness. After discerning that the LORD was not in the mighty wind, nor in the earthquake, nor in the fire, he discovered the LORD in a *still, small voice.*

Those who have not requested the Lord to *take away my* [own] *life, for I am not better than my fathers,* continue to think they will find the fullness of God in the effusion of the gifts of God in the mighty wind of His Spirit, or in the earthquake of revival when many are turning to the Lord Jesus, or in the fire of God's judgment on others. Yet they never discover that the fullness and perfection of knowing the Lord is *only in the still, small voice* of an intimate, hearing relationship with Him in the realm of His life (for it is *Christ in you, the hope of glory*).

Therefore, they fall into the trap of becoming careless. Instead of concentrating on hearing the still, small voice, they follow after circumstances (miracles and provision and open doors), mistaking this for the voice of the Lord. They are unaware that the only place of safety and security is in the *secret place of the most high.*

The true goal of all who are called to be spiritual fathers in the Lord, such as the case with the first-century apostles, is to join others to Christ that He might bring them unto His Father. For He said unto them *Suffer the little children to come unto me and forbid them not* and *no one comes unto the Father, but by me.* Paul said that he was in travail that he might present the Corinthians as a *chaste virgin unto Christ.*

The generation that died in the wilderness continued to be led by the pillar of cloud by day and the pillar of fire by night. The manna of God's miraculous provision was there without fail every morning. But even though God revealed His miraculous *acts* to them, they died in the wilderness, short of their promised inheritance, because they failed to pay the price (death to their own ways) so that they might learn His *ways* (Psalm 103:7). They said unto Moses *Speak thou with us, and we will hear, but let not God speak with us lest we die* (Exodus 20:19).

To continue to personally hear the voice of the Lord will ultimately cost us everything. If, in search of an easier way, we start to follow the circumstances of the *acts* of God (His miracles and provision and the revelation He has given to others) instead of the still, small voice, our old selves will become revived and take the credit for what God is doing. We run a terrible risk every time we take our eyes off of Jesus Christ and begin to admire our own self.

This was how King David, a man after God's heart, lost his intimate relationship with God and fell into such sin as adultery and murder. This was how Moses, the meekest man on the face of the earth, fell into the sin of pride and presumption. This was how Elijah, who one day prayed and God answered by fire, came to flee the wrath of Jezebel the next day like a coward. To sin when we know better (even in the thoughts of our heart) is always very costly. Yet, as David and Moses and Elijah discovered, there is a way back into intimate fellowship with God, and that way, God's way, is through the fire of the dealings of God until the old man is completely dead.

> 4 *For it is impossible that those who once received the light and tasted of that heavenly gift* [the life of the Lord Jesus Christ who is the gift sent from heaven] *and were made partakers of the Holy Spirit* [receiving the gifts, anointing, and revelation of the Spirit],

5 *and likewise have tasted the good word of God* [heard His voice] *and the virtue of the age to come* [a taste of the kingdom of God],

6 *and have backslidden* [back into their own devices], *be renewed again by repentance, crucifying again for themselves* [selfish purposes] *the Son of God* [that they might use His power to build their own kingdoms] *and putting him to an open shame* [because their lives do not back up their message; therefore they cannot be renewed a second time through repentance by promising to keep a covenant with God; they can only be restored through actual compliance with the covenant by submitting to the fire of His dealings until they are actually dead to sin].

7 *For the earth which drinks in the rain* [man who was made from the dust of the earth and drinks in the provision of God] *that comes often upon it* [him] *and brings forth herbs* [good fruit] *in season for those by whom it is dressed* [Jesus and His Father and those in union with them whom they send], *receives blessing from God* [only those who bear good fruit that measured up to God's standards will receive the fullness of God's blessing];

8 *But that which bears thorns and briers is rejected* [the kingdom of self and all its works] *and is near unto cursing* [unless self is surrendered voluntarily], *whose end shall be by fire* [at the appointed time for judgment without mercy, unless we submit voluntarily to the fire of the intimate dealings of God in the tabernacle of David while there is still His provision for judgment with mercy].

9 *But, beloved, we expect better things than these of you* [that you will allow God to deal with self], *things near unto saving* [from the power and dominion of self] *health, though we thus speak* (Hebrews 6:4-9).

In the original language, 1 Kings 19:4 actually reads *take away my soul* instead of *take away my life.* This means that it was not just referring to the *deeds of the flesh,* which had already been dealt with in Elijah. He was a man who could say *I have done all these things at thy word,* demonstrating perfect obedience to God. Rather, this was a death to all his own dreams, ambitions, desires, and emotions regarding ministry in his own right.

The name *Elijah* means either "the LORD is God", which had already been clearly demonstrated in the ministry of Elijah on Mount Carmel in direct confrontation with the prophets of Baal, or *Elijah* means "God Himself", which is what Elijah would manifest from this time forward. Elijah, as a manifestation of *God Himself* in and through a human prophet, would walk right through the Jordan of death on dry ground and be *caught up to God and to his throne* in a whirlwind.

Elijah is a type and shadow of a prophetic company of overcomers (dead to sin) who will manifest God Himself as they live and proclaim *this gospel of the kingdom ... in all the world for a witness* (Matthew 24:14) before the end of the church age shall come. They shall prepare the way for the second coming of the Lord and for the full restoration of the glory of the kingdom of God on the earth (Malachi 4:4-6; Matthew 17:11; Mark 9:11-12; Luke 1:17).

The transfiguration was a preview of the glory of the kingdom of God in which two companies of overcomers will be transformed and joined to Jesus Christ to reign and rule with Him for a thousand years following the first resurrection.

14 For if we believe that Jesus died and rose again, even so those who sleep in Jesus [who are dead to sin in Jesus] *will God also bring with him.*

15 For this, we say unto you by the word of the Lord, that we who are alive and remain [the Elijah company of overcomers] *unto the coming of the Lord shall not precede* [come before] *those who are asleep* [in Jesus, the Moses company of overcomers].

16 For the Lord himself shall descend from heaven with a shout, with the voice of the archangel [the corporate angel with the message of the eternal gospel of the kingdom], *and with the trumpet of God* [the seventh trumpet]; *and the dead in Christ shall rise first* [the Moses company of the overcomers who have gone on before];

17 Then we who are alive and remain [the Elijah company of overcomers who shall walk right through death into the glory of the kingdom] *shall be caught up together* [to God and to His throne or authority] *with them* [the Moses company] *in the clouds* [the coming storm of God's righteous judgment upon the earth], *to meet the Lord in the air* [this word *air* means natural or ambient air and comes from the root *to breathe*], *and so shall we ever be with the Lord* [as His kingdom comes on earth even as it is in heaven] (1 Thessalonians 4:14-17).

4 And I saw thrones, and those who sat upon them, and judgment was given unto them; and I saw the souls of those that were beheaded for the witness of Jesus [those who willingly relinquished their own headship to come under His exclusive headship; we do not rule out those who were literally beheaded for the cause of Christ] *and for the word of God and who had not worshipped the beast* [the Adamic nature of man in any of its manifestations, be it the "beast" of self-rule within or the ultimate Antichrist attempting world government or any other type of worship of man] *neither its image* [religion honoring or worshipping man along with God], *neither had received its mark upon their foreheads* [man's way of thinking] *or in their hands* [man's way of doing]; *and they shall live and reign with Christ* [as part of a corporate overcomer] *the thousand years.*

5 *But the rest of the dead* [those who did not die to sin and overcome in the power of the Lord] *did not live again until the thousand years were finished. This is the first resurrection* [many complacent Christians, who did not press on into their inheritance of victory in Christ within and without, will die and not wake up until the general resurrection at the end of the thousand years].

6 *Blessed and holy is he that has part in the first resurrection; on such the second death has no authority, but they shall be priests of God and of the Christ and shall reign with him a thousand years* (Revelation 20:4-6).

It is interesting to note that both Elisha and Joshua went above and beyond their human teachers (Elijah and Moses), indicating that the human ministry they received was indeed successful in joining them unto the Lord. They were indeed taught and fathered by Him. Yet, even though Joshua was the one chosen to lead the children of

Israel into the Promised Land in victory, and Elisha received a double portion of the spirit of Elijah and lived to see the defeat of Jezebel, it was Elijah and Moses who had the honor of speaking with Jesus on the Mount of Transfiguration in the glory of the kingdom.

Yet the purpose of the transfiguration preview of the glory of the kingdom was not to lift up Moses and Elijah; rather it was to:

1 *consider the Apostle and High Priest of our profession, Christ Jesus,*

2 *who was faithful to him that appointed him over all his house, as also Moses was faithful.*

3 *For this man was counted worthy of more glory than Moses, inasmuch as he* [the Lord Jesus Christ] *who has built the house has more honour than the house* [Moses, Elijah, John the Baptist, and the rest of those who overcome] (Hebrews 3:1-3).

The only way to participate in the government of the kingdom of God is to die to sin. Another way of stating this is to *enter into his rest.*

4 *For he spoke in a certain place of the seventh day like this, And God rested the seventh day from all his works.*

5 *And in this place again, They shall not enter into my rest.*

6 *Seeing, therefore, it remains that some must enter therein, and those to whom it was first preached did not enter in because of disobedience;*

7 *Again, he determines a certain day, saying* [in the past and again in the restored tabernacle of David], *Today, by David so long a time afterward; as it is said, Today* [because tomorrow the opportunity may be irrevocably gone] *if ye*

will hear his voice, harden not your hearts [do not refuse to let God have control of your will].

8 *For if Jesus had given them rest, then he would not afterward have spoken of another day.* [This is a reference to Joshua (the Hebrew name which is the same as *Jesus* in Greek), but it is also true that although the merit of the death of Jesus can bring us back into fellowship with God, it will not give us automatic entrance into God's rest. For, even though *we were reconciled with God by the death of his Son, much more, now reconciled, we shall be saved by his life* (Romans 5:10). Our salvation is conditional on allowing the life of God to flow through us at the expense of our own, for we are saved by His life.]

9 *There remains therefore a rest for the people of God* [those who have agreed to God's covenant through identification in the death and resurrection of the Lord Jesus Christ].

10 *For he that is entered into his rest, he also has ceased from his own works* [actually complied with God's covenant and completely dead to sin and fully alive in Christ, ceasing from his own works], *as God did from his.* [After the initial creation, God did not force Adam to obey him; He rested and allowed Adam to choose. And after becoming a new creation in Christ, we are not forced by God to go on with Him; we are free to take our newfound life and gifts and use them to attempt to further His kingdom our own way (which will undoubtedly glorify man), or we can lay them at His feet and submit even to the death of that which we consider to be good in our own selves if He should so command. Jesus rested in the will of His Father even unto

death on the cross, choosing not to become an earthly Messiah in His own right.]

11 *Let us therefore make haste to enter into that rest* [we will have to put all of our attention, will, and effort into hearing and obeying the voice of God even though it will cost us our ability to act and operate on our own apart from Him], *lest anyone fall after the same example of disobedience.*

12 *For the word of God is alive, and efficient and sharper than any twoedged sword, piercing even to the dividing asunder of soul and spirit* [to reveal and to separate what is of us (soul) from what is of God (Spirit)], *and of the joints and marrow* [to expose the means and motivation behind the horizontal joining that is going on today among those using the name of Christ], *and is a discerner of the thoughts and intents of the heart* [no matter how much we rationalize and explain away our besetting sins (be they individual or corporate), He can see right through all of it].

13 *Neither is there any created thing that is not manifested in his presence, but all things are naked and opened unto the eyes of him of whom we speak* [so He is well able to cleanse and perfect us].

14 *Having, therefore, a great high priest who penetrated the heavens, Jesus the Son of God, let us hold fast this profession of our hope* [death to our own way (self) that we might go His way (life) and find our existence in union with the Lord Jesus Christ].

15 *For we do not have a high priest who cannot sympathize with our weaknesses, but was in all points tempted like as*

we are, yet without sin. [The Lord Jesus has a very special place in His heart for us and is highly motivated to bring us up to His level.]

16 *Let us, therefore, come boldly unto the throne of his grace* [for judgment with mercy in the tabernacle of David of the intimate and direct dealings of God in our lives], *that we may obtain mercy, and find grace to help in time of need* [the power of the grace of God not only to forgive our sin *but to cleanse us from all unrighteousness*] (Hebrews 4:4-16).

We are almost to the start of the seventh millennium (the seventh prophetical thousand-year day) from creation (2 Peter 3:8). When this happens, there are many types and shadows in Scripture to suggest that a major change will occur, and that God and His overcomers will enter into a corporate rest in which His power, gifts, and anointing will not be available for use outside of perfect union with Him. Now the Spirit is available to be poured out on *all flesh.* That is, all we have to do is agree (not comply) to the covenant, and He will give us of His life and of the gifts of His Spirit.

The prize of the high calling awaits those who learn to hear His voice and follow and obey until the covenant is a reality, and they are really dead to sin and alive to Him. On the other hand, those who use the gifts and blessings of God for their own selfish purposes will be rudely awakened someday to find that the *today* that Scripture mentions is over, and they have lost their chance to enter into the intimate fullness of the kingdom with the Lord Jesus Christ and His overcomers.

1 *Then shall the kingdom of the heavens be likened unto ten virgins who, taking their lamps* [the gifts, revelation, and

life in the Spirit that God had given them], *went forth to meet the bridegroom.*

2 *And five of them were prudent, and five were foolish.*

3 *Those that were foolish took their lamps and took no oil with them;*

4 *But the prudent took oil in their vessels* [they had allowed themselves to be cleansed inside and filled with the nature and purpose of God, instead of with the nature and purpose of their own natural selves] *with their lamps* (Matthew 25:1-4).

At the present time, all the *lamps* look similar. But there is a feature that will only become apparent at the midnight hour when the oil runs out for those who do not have a reservoir of the oil of God's desire, design, and purpose permeating their entire being or vessel. There is a time coming when the gifts and anointing of the Holy Spirit that is available to all flesh will run out. Then only those who are tapped into the overcoming body of Christ, which has an unlimited anointing flowing from the head to each member of the body, will shine. Only those who have paid the price (their whole self) to come exclusively under His headship will shine. It will be too late to buy more oil, because the offer that God is making *today* to those who hear His voice will be over, and His new day will have begun.

Many are confused and deceived by the desires of their own hearts in this present hour, because it is still possible to follow the desires of our own hearts and continue to flow in the power and anointing of the gifts and revelation that God has given us. But a great change is about to take place at the midnight hour when the lamps of those who do not have oil in their vessels will start to go out.

Those who are dependent on their God-given gifts and abilities, or on revelation that they have acquired from books written by anointed men of God (even from the Bible), or on revelation, guidance, council, or covering from anointed human ministry, will find that their lamps will go out. The true purpose of gifts, revelation, and ministry is that we and others might know Him, and the power of His resurrection, and the fellowship of His sufferings, being made conformable unto His death (Philippians 3:10). And while the foolish are wandering around in the dark attempting to buy oil, those who have oil in their vessels, being *partakers of the divine nature, having escaped the corruption that is in the world through lust* [the insatiable desires of self] (2 Peter 1:4), will enter into the kingdom and the door will be shut.

> 21 *Not everyone that saith unto me, Lord, Lord, shall enter into the kingdom of heaven* [even though those who call Him their Lord can receive gifts, revelation, power, and guidance from Him for a season]; *but* [only] *he that doeth* [actually complies with] *the will of my Father which is in heaven* [shall enter in].

> 22 *Many will say to me in that day* [the day of the Lord], *Lord, Lord, have we not prophesied* [even giving great revelation] *in thy name? and in thy name have cast out devils* [with power and authority from you]? *and in thy name done many wonderful works* [including miracles]?

> 23 *And then will I profess unto them, I never knew you: depart from me, ye that work iniquity* [when the gifts, revelation, and power of God are used for the promotion and gain of our own selves, instead of for the death of our desires and appetites that He might shine forth in us, God calls

it iniquity and will not have it in His kingdom] (Matthew 7:21-23).

Anyone who is forced to say to the Lord, "Look what we have done in your name (v. 22)," is promoting a corporate self that in reality is an abomination before the Lord. Sometimes we can be fooled into thinking that because we seem to have given up our own way so the purposes of our corporate group or community can prevail, we have died to sin. But in reality, we have only exchanged our individual sin for corporate sin. That may be even harder to put to death because the wills of many others are involved.

If we are dead to sin individually and corporately, then God is our justifier, and we will have no need to promote ourselves to anyone by saying, "Look what we have done in the name of the Lord." The fact that we may have great revelation, that we may have engaged in successful spiritual warfare, and that we may have done many *wonderful works* in His name will not stop the Lord from labeling it all iniquity and casting us out of His presence if it turns out that we have been using His name to promote ourselves. For *he that soweth iniquity shall reap vanity* [or nothing] (Proverbs 22:8).

3 *For anyone thinks himself to be something, when he is nothing, he deceives himself.*

4 *But let everyone prove his own work* [by the fruit of it, whether it be of the flesh or of the Spirit], *and then he shall have glory regarding only himself* [the fruit of the Spirit being manifested individually], *and not in another* [the fact that we belong to the right group, believe the right message, or receive the right ministry will not guarantee the fruit of the Spirit in our lives].

5 *For everyone shall bear his own burden* [no matter what group we are part of, or what human ministry we appreciate and look up to, we are all individually responsible before the Lord, and our security must be in Him and not in our group or in our doctrine].

6 *Let the one that is taught in the word communicate* [share in everything] *unto the one that teacheth in all good things* [the only one who truly teaches in all good things is God (either directly or through ministry that He has truly sent), so we should freely share everything we have (including ourselves) with God if we are being taught by Him].

7 *Do not deceive yourselves* [if we think that we are really something when in God's eyes we are nothing, we will be deceived]; *God is not mocked: for whatever a man sows, that shall he also reap* (Galatians 6:3-7).

If God created man in His image and pronounced this creative work *very good*, how is it that we must die to our natural self? Does God want to destroy our personality? Does God want to destroy that which He created to be very good?

29 *Behold , this only have I found, that God hath made man upright; but they have sought out many perversions* (Ecclesiastes 7:29).

The truth in this matter is that God never created man to be his own moral agent. It is true that God put man in the garden and gave him dominion over the earth, but God prohibited man from partaking of one thing in all of creation. In order to remain in fellowship with God and retain dominion over the earth, man must never eat *of the tree of the knowledge of good and evil ... for in the day that thou dost eat of it thou shalt surely die* [be separated from God who is the only source of life] (Genesis 2:17).

In order to come back into eternal fellowship with God, man must die to having his own way. He must give up his right to the knowledge of good and evil. He must let God be the one to have absolute control over what is right and wrong. Contrary to popular belief, this death to sin, this death to any future possibility of erecting a kingdom of self, is the only way to experience the true realization of our personality, our individuality, and the uniqueness of the creative work of God in us. This is the only way to come to maturity as a son of God, qualified to be a joint heir with Jesus Christ to reign and rule with Him for all eternity.

God builds His true temple with living stones, each one created and formed under the hand of God to be a unique expression of His artistic touch, and each one cemented to another by the golden nature of God Himself. It is in Babylon where human bricks are stamped out in a mold (as exactly alike as possible) by the control and institutions of man and held together by the slime (instead of mortar) of humanism (worship of man).

It has not been hard to get God's people to acknowledge the need to return the knowledge of evil back into the hands of God. Many turn to God and cry out for deliverance in the depths of crisis caused by bondage to a known evil that goes directly against the law of God. The problem has always been with the knowledge of good. This is because what we think is good is sometimes evil in the sight of God, and what He thinks is good sometimes appears evil to our natural mind. Until we have died to sin, we find it very difficult to see things from God's point of view, making it impossible for us to perceive His ultimate purpose for mankind.

Yet, even in the midst of the struggles, turmoil, and tribulations of this natural life, God gives us this measuring stick: *so that by their fruits ye shall know them* (Matthew 7:20). He did not say by their doctrine, their message, their gifts, or by their revelation, but *by their fruits ye shall know them*. There are only two fruits that we need to differentiate: (1) the evil fruit that comes from a corrupt tree, and (2) the good fruit that comes from a good tree (Matthew 20:16-20).

The source of the evil tree is self-rule. Evil entered the world by the decision of Adam to take the *knowledge of good and evil* for himself. This fruit is summed up in the kingdoms of self or the kingdoms of this world.

The source of the good tree is the rule of God, and the fruit is the permanence of the kingdom of God in each individual who dies to sin (only then can we be properly joined, without leaven, to one another). The day is now on the horizon when the kingdoms of self shall fail, and *the kingdoms of this world are become the Kingdom of our Lord and of His Christ.*

> 1 *Thus hath the Lord God showed unto me: and behold a basket of summer fruit* [Sooner or later, in the proper season, the fruit of those calling themselves by the name of the Lord is manifest].
>
> 2 *And he said, Amos, what seest thou? And I said, A basket of summer fruit. Then said the LORD unto me, The end is come upon my people of Israel* [God's judgment is always based on the fruit. In this case He took one look at the fruit, pronounced an end to His protection and said]; *I will not again pass over them any more* (Amos 8:1-2).

This is a reference to the Passover (Exodus 12:1-12) in which He would pass over those who had killed a sacrificial lamb that was without blemish and had applied the blood to the doorposts of their house (self) in identification with the death of Christ. They had to eat bread without leaven (feed on what God says without listening to man) and consume all the flesh of the lamb after roasting it in the fire (take the entire message of the gospel and not leave out the parts they didn't like).

With their staff in their hand (ready to submit to the discipline and dealings of God), their loins girded (their desire to father spiritual children held in check until they were perfected and mature in the Lord), and their sandals on (in readiness to walk in the Spirit), they followed the pillar of cloud and the pillar of fire through the *baptism unto Moses* (a type of Christ) *and in the cloud* (a type of the Holy Spirit) *and all passed through the* (Red) *sea* (sealing their covenant with God) (1 Corinthians 10:1-15). They passed through all the dealings of God in the wilderness until they came to actual death to sin (circumcision of the heart) when they passed through the Jordan River prior to entering their inheritance in God.

The Passover was conditional and temporal. As long as God was able to deal with and perfect His people under the terms of the covenant, He would pass over and not judge the sin and imperfection remaining in His people. However, at the end of the set time of His dealings, at harvest time, when He, as the gardener, is expecting good fruit, if the fruit should turn out to be unacceptable, He will refuse to pass over any longer; judgment will fall similar to what fell on the Egyptians, *for He is no respecter of persons.*

> 9 *And it shall come to pass in that day, said the Lord God,*
> *that I will cause the sun to go down at noon* [at the zenith
> of the kingdoms of man], *and I will cover the earth with*
> *darkness in the clear day* [the light from all the blessings

and giftings of God will abruptly cease for those who glorify man in any way instead of God].

10 *And I will turn your feasts* [notice He says *your* feasts instead of *My* feasts of Passover (redemption), Pentecost (effusion of the Spirit), and Tabernacles (fullness and harvest) done man's way (Leviticus 23)] *into mourning and all your songs into lamentations* [all your praise and worship done with unclean hands and hearts that only serve to lift up your souls to vanity, attempting to anesthetize your conscience and cover up your deceit], *and I will cause sackcloth to be brought upon all loins* [the spiritual promiscuity of using the blessings, giftings, and revelation of God to achieve man's goals will be exposed for what it is, producing repentance and shame], *and baldness upon every head* [the glory will totally depart from the kingdoms under the headship of self]; *and I will make it as the mourning of an only son* [The death angel killed the firstborn, the heirs to each household among the Egyptians, on the Passover while God's people were temporarily spared (Exodus 12:13); now the tables will be turned and the heirs to the kingdoms of self among the people of God will be destroyed], *and the end thereof as a bitter day.*

11 *Behold, the days come, said the Lord God that I will send a famine to the earth, not a famine of bread, nor a thirst for water, but of hearing the words of the LORD:*

12 *And they shall wander from sea to sea, and from north even to the east, they shall run to and fro to seek the word of the LORD, and shall not find it* [those who depend on their gifting and on the ministry and revelation of others will

not be able to hear from the Lord, no matter how desperate they get].

13 *In that day shall the fair* [and foolish] *virgins and young men* [those who have failed to come to maturity in Christ in the time allotted them] *faint for thirst* (Amos 8:9-13).

At that time of *great tribulation such as the world has never known,* God will have sons who have come to maturity in Christ. He will have a company of overcomers who have completely died to sin and will manifest the fullness of *this gospel of the Kingdom* according to the pattern. The Lord Jesus Christ is the pattern, and He did not do anything on His own apart from manifesting the perfect will of His Father. After the glory and light of the kingdoms of self that have been built in His name have gone completely dark, after the lamps of the foolish virgins go out, after gross darkness covers the earth, they will *behold the glory of the God of Israel ... and his noise was like a noise of many waters* [many overcomers]: *and the earth shined with his glory* (Ezekiel 43:2).

Yes, God is building a house, a *temple made without hands,* to be *an holy habitation unto himself.* This house will not be leavened with man's plans, man's ways, or even man's good intentions. Sin will have no place here. Only those who have died to sin and found their eternal existence in Him will form part of this temple. When He is ready and the world is in the depths of darkness and despair, the glory of God will fill this house built from the individual stones that have been carefully prepared in the tabernacle of David. When God begins to assemble His true temple, it will be awesome.

1 *And I saw, and, behold, a Lamb* [in total meekness and submission to do only the will of God] *stood on the mount Sion* [the mountain of His holiness], *and* [the dressing of

individual stones according to the dealings of God in the tabernacle of David has progressed to the point in time where there are now] *with him an hundred forty and four thousand, having the name of his Father written in their foreheads* [that have died to their own way and live only to manifest the Father, just like Jesus, the pattern Son].

2 *And I heard a voice from heaven, as the voice of many waters, and as the voice of a great thunder: and I heard the voice of harpers harping with their harps* [the harps of God, the true praise that comes only from walking in victory]:

3 *and they sang as it were a new song before the throne* [but in reality, it is an old song, the song of Moses, the song of the Lamb, the song of death to sin (Deuteronomy 32; Revelation 15:3)], *and before the four animals, and the elders: and no one* [still living under the control of self] *could learn that song but the hundred and forty and four thousand, who were redeemed from the earth.*

4 *These are those who are not defiled with women* [they did not use their gifts, calling, ministry, and revelation promiscuously to build the kingdoms of self]; *for they are virgins. These are those that follow the Lamb* [in meekness] *wherever he goes. These are redeemed from among men, being the firstfruits unto God and to the Lamb* [they belong totally to God and to the Lamb].

5 *And in their mouth was found no guile* [*if any man offend not in word, the same is a perfect man ... but the tongue can no man tame* (James 3:2, 8). Therefore these are dead to sin, to the desires, ambitions, and appetites of man, and alive

only to God, being partakers of the divine nature]: *for they are without blemish before the throne of God.*

6 And I saw another angel fly in the midst of heaven, having the eternal gospel that he might evangelize those that dwell on the earth, and every nation, and kindred, and tongue, and people (Revelation 14:1-6).

Let us take a closer look at this *everlasting gospel* or *gospel of the kingdom* that will be lived and preached to all that dwell on the earth through a company of overcomers in whose mouth there is no guile and who are without fault before the throne of God. This is the message that God speaks forth in and through them:

6 And I heard him speaking unto me out of the house

7 And he said unto me, Son of man, this is the place of my throne [or authority], *and the place of the soles of my feet* [of those I have truly sent], *in which I will dwell in the midst of the sons of Israel forever, and my holy name, the house of Israel shall* [those who are called by my name] *no longer defile, neither they, nor their kings* [their self-rule], *by their whoredom* [promiscuous use of my name, gifts, and revelation to build their own kingdoms], *nor by the carcasses of their kings* [dead works and abominations of self] *in their altars* [in the kingdoms they have erected where they call the people to worship in my name but according to their own ways].

8 In their setting of their threshold by my thresholds [they make the people think they are entering my kingdom when in reality, they are entering a man-made kingdom], *and their post by my posts* [God's posts or columns are called *Jaquim* (He will establish) and *Boaz* (in Him only is strength); man's posts are called *we will establish* and *in us is strength* (2 Chronicles 3:17)] *and a wall between me and them* [there is an insurmountable wall between these two positions], *they have even defiled my holy name by their abominations that they have committed* [by using the gifts of power and revelation from God in such a promiscuous manner according to the whims of self, that it has brought great dishonor to His name even before the heathen]: *therefore I have consumed them in mine anger.*

9 *Now let them put away their whoredom* [no man can serve two masters], *and the carcasses of their kings* [the dead works of their selfish abominations], *far from me, and I will dwell in the midst of them forever* [note that this verse is conditional].

10 *Thou son of man, show this* [true and undefiled] *house to the* [defiled] *house of* [spiritual] *Israel* [that man has built in my name calling it my church], *that they may be ashamed of their iniquities: and let them understand the pattern* [Jesus Christ as sovereign LORD is that pattern].

11 *And if they are ashamed of all that they have done, show them the form of the house* [how God joins His true people together], *and its pattern* [God's purpose for mankind], *and the goings out thereof, and the comings in thereof* [the true liberty and freedom of being dead to sin and alive in Christ], *and all its figures* [everything that has to be dealt with in us so that we can truly be free in Christ], *and all its descriptions* [God's way of doing things], *and all its paintings* [all the aspects of walking in the glorious inheritance of the

sons of God], *and all its laws* [the law of the Spirit of life
(Romans 8:2), the law of liberty (James 1:25; 2:12)]: *and write*
it in their sight, that they may keep the whole form thereof
[that they may be patterned after Jesus Christ], *and all the*
ordinances thereof [that they may learn His ways], *and do*
them (Ezekiel 43:6-11).

God's people are guilty of building the house of the Lord their own
way. They are guilty of preaching a *first feast* or *outer court* gospel
of easy believism that promises safety and security in exchange for
acknowledgment of historical facts and a head knowledge of doctrine.
They preach this instead of preaching repentance from going our own
way and faith in Jesus Christ as Lord who can change, purify, perfect,
and consume us so that we might truly go His way.

The baptism in the Holy Spirit or Feast of Pentecost is then preached
to those who have bypassed the cross and all that it represents,
resulting in the use of the gifts, anointing, power, and revelation of
the Spirit for the furthering of man's kingdoms – instead of using
them for the true purpose for which they were given – to perfect us
and deliver us from bondage to ourselves and the systems of man
that have been erected in the name of God.

With this kind of abomination going on in the holy place, many add
to it by preaching a version of the third feast (the Feast of Tabernacles)
that has also been leavened by man. Instead of recognizing the need
to stop and start according to the perfect will of God, they try to fit
their vision of the third feast on top of the perverted first and second
feasts. This results in a number of difficulties, such as the carelessness
that comes from the doctrine of ultimate, or universal, reconciliation.
This extreme form erroneously insists – contrary to Scripture – that

everyone including the devil will eventually be saved (Revelation 20:10-15).

But in and through all the confusion generated by the various manifestations of sin, God is still steadily at work in the tabernacle of David, perfecting and dressing each individual stone that will pay the price of submission to His intimate dealings by hearing and obeying His still small voice (2 Samuel 6; Isaiah 16:5; Amos 9:11; Acts 15:16). Obedience to that voice is costly. It will cause many to be *wounded in the house of their friends*. It will eventually cause all that hear and obey that voice to die to sin (Romans 6:2) if we do not shy away from the fire of His dealings.

> 5 *Hear the word of the LORD, ye that tremble at his word;*
> *Your brethren that hate you, that deny you for my name's*
> *sake, said, Let the LORD be glorified: but he shall appear to*
> *your joy, and they shall be ashamed.*

> 6 *A voice of noise from the city* [of religion], *a voice from the*
> *temple* [of the judgment that begins in the house of God], *a*
> *voice of the LORD that rendereth recompense to his enemies.*

> 7 *Before she travailed, she brought forth; before her pain came,*
> *she was delivered of a manchild* [a corporate overcomer].

> 8 *Who hath heard of such a thing? who hath seen such things?*
> *Shall the earth bring forth in one day? Shall an entire nation*
> *be born at once? that Zion travailed, and shall bring forth*
> *her sons together?*

> 9 *I, who make births to happen, shall I not be with child?*
> *saith the LORD: I, who cause conception, shall I be stopped?*
> *saith thy God.*

10 *Rejoice ye with Jerusalem* [the Jerusalem from above that is the mother of us all], *and be glad with her, all ye that love her: be filled with joy with her, all ye that mourn for her:*

11 *That ye may suck, and be satisfied with the breasts of her consolations; that ye may milk out, and be delighted with the splendor of her glory.*

12 *For thus saith the LORD, Behold I will extend peace to her like a river, and the glory of the Gentiles like a flowing stream: then shall ye suck, ye shall be borne upon her sides, and be dandled upon her knees.*

13 *As a man child whom his mother comforts, so will I comfort you; and ye shall be comforted in Jerusalem.*

14 *And ye shall see, your heart shall rejoice, and your bones shall flourish like grass: and the hand of the LORD shall be known toward his servants, and his indignation towards his enemies* (Isaiah 66:5-14).

The True Meaning of the Lord's Supper

26 For each time that ye eat this bread and drink this cup, ye declare the Lord's death until he comes (1 Corinthians 11:26).

When we feed on what God says and *eat this bread* of the living Word (which will also quicken the written Word to us), instead of feeding on what man says, or listening to what Satan says, and when we *drink this cup* of death to sin and of life in Christ, we *declare the Lord's death until he comes.*

The time has come when the Lord is restoring the truth regarding both water baptism and the Lord's Supper to the people of God. The new covenant that God would make with us requires our signature and His to be valid. If we truly repent of going our own way and wish to die to sin and live under the rule of Christ, our signature on the covenant is water baptism – to publicly demonstrate our repentance and faith. His signature (if He approves of the terms of the covenant we have signed) is to baptize us in the Holy Spirit and fire.

In the book of Acts, when someone was baptized in water, they normally received the baptism of the Holy Spirit by the laying on of hands at the same time, indicating God's signature of the covenant along with their own. Tragically, as church history progressed, God quit signing the covenant as baptism took on the meaning of entering the kingdoms of man as a rite of membership into a given denominated church instead of into Christ.

The communion of the Lord's Supper became a tool of man to horizontally join those who for the most part were never truly joined to the Lord. It is extremely rare in our present day and age to see anyone baptized in the Holy Spirit at the time of water baptism. Or for that person to experience the *circumcision of Christ* as the fire of the Holy Spirit cuts the control of the flesh, the world, and the religious traditions of men, placing the person under the direct control of the Lord Jesus Christ – that they might immediately begin to walk with Him in victory, as was the case with so many during the first three centuries of the church. Anything less than this leaves Satan with his foot in the door, ready to exercise his rights over anything that has not been totally surrendered to the Lord Jesus Christ.

The true meaning of the Lord's Supper is that whenever we would have fellowship in Christ around natural food and drink, He would have us remember and ratify our covenant with Him – to be dead to the sin of our own ways and appetites and be alive in Him (with a newfound *hunger and thirst for righteousness*). We are to feed only on the bread of what He says, and we are to drink the wine of new life in Christ, which means death to our old life. If this is not the case, we should abstain from the natural food until any unfinished business between the Lord and us, or between one another, is resolved.

> 27 *Therefore whoever shall eat this bread, and drink this cup of the Lord, unworthily, shall be guilty of the body and blood of the Lord.*

> 28 *But let each man prove himself, and so let him eat of the bread, and drink of the cup.*

29 For he that eats and drinks unworthily, eats and drinks judgment to himself, not discerning the Lord's body.

30 For this cause many are weak and sickly among you, and many sleep.

31 For if we would examine ourselves, we should not be judged.

32 But being judged we are chastened of the Lord, that we should not be condemned with the world (1 Corinthians 11:27-32).

The kingdoms of men who have attempted to control others through exclusiveness regarding water baptism and the Lord's Supper are full of those who are *weak and sickly ... and many sleep.* This is true both in the natural realm and in the spiritual realm. Therefore let us *judge ourselves;* let us judge our individual and corporate selves that we might be *chastened of the Lord, that we should not be condemned with the world.*

The time is at hand when the Lord shall restore the full significance of water baptism and the Lord's Supper as key times when the natural and spiritual meet and fulfill His promise that:

18 Whatsoever ye shall bind on earth shall be bound in heaven: and whatsoever ye shall loose on earth shall be loosed in heaven.

19 Again I say unto you, That if two of you shall agree on earth as touching anything that they shall ask, it shall be done for them of my Father which is in heaven.

20 For where two or three are gathered together in my name [instead of in their own individual or corporate names], *there am I in the midst of them* (Matthew 18:18-20).

17 *For I will take away the names of Baals* [of other lords and masters] *out of her mouth* [speaking of the bride of Christ], *and they* [the individual members of this corporate bride] *shall no longer be remembered by their* [own] *name.*

18 *And in that time will I make a covenant for them with the beasts of the field, and with the fowls of heaven, and with the serpents of the earth: and I will break the bow and the sword and the battle of the earth, and will cause them to sleep safely* [this is the day when God shall *repent* Himself for His people and deliver them from all their enemies that they might serve Him without fear all the days of their lives].

19 *And I will betroth thee unto me forever; yea, I will betroth thee unto me in righteousness, and in judgment, and in mercy.*

20 *I will even betroth thee unto me in faith: and thou shalt know the LORD.*

21 *And it shall come to pass in that day, I will respond, saith the LORD, I will respond to the heavens* [those who make their abode in Christ], *and they shall respond to the earth* [the people of God who cry out for deliverance];

22 *And the earth shall respond to the wheat* [that falls into the ground and dies], *and the wine* [of new life in Christ], *and the oil* [the anointing, flowing from the true body of Christ]; *and they shall respond to Jezreel* [God shall plant this gospel of the kingdom His way in an overcoming bride who has died to sin].

23 *And I will sow her unto me in the earth; and I will have mercy upon Loruhamah,* [those who are wandering in the world outside the church, confused and perplexed by the

hypocrisy and disorder among those claiming to represent God], *Thou art my people; and he shall say, Thou art my God* [there shall be a response to the gospel as never before when it is lived and proclaimed according to God's perfect will by a people who are willing to lay down their own lives] (Hosea 2:17-23).

10 *And I heard a loud voice saying in heaven, Now is come salvation, and virtue, and the kingdom of our God, and the power of his Christ: for the accuser of our brethren is cast down, who accused them before our God day and night.*

11 *And they have overcome him by the blood of the Lamb, and by the word of their testimony; and they loved not their lives unto the death* (Revelation 12:10-11).

RUSSELL M. STENDAL

THE
TEMPLE

*Rebuilding the temple of God with a
clean word, received by a clean people*

The Temple

*Rebuilding the temple of God
with a clean word, received by a clean people*

Russell M. Stendal

LIFE SENTENCE
——Publishing, LLC——

The Temple

The Old Testament books from Ezra to Job are interesting, because this is the story of a remnant of Israel returning from Babylon to rebuild Jerusalem and the temple of the Lord. We need to understand that we are the temple of the Lord, but we are not the whole temple as individuals. This temple is formed by many living stones that are united by God's nature, and a temple of this magnitude, made God's way, has never been seen on earth, nor has there been a temple (a group of people) in which the Lord is flowing with purity.

The greatest thing we have seen are individuals who have walked in this way with the Lord; however, there has never been a group that the Lord has been able to show to the world and say, "These are my people." The examples that we have seen from Christian groups have been marked with faults and problems, so much so that many people (many theologians) teach that it is impossible for there ever to be a perfect manifestation of God in a people. But the Bible says the complete opposite. It says that the Lord will return for a clean bride, without stain and without a wrinkle, and we are this bride.

It is important to remember that when the people of God as a group are spoken of in the Bible, they are referred to in the feminine gender. God is referred to as masculine. On the other hand, when God speaks of our individual dealings with Him, He speaks of us as if we were His sons, using the masculine gender, because the Lord wants to do something in us that will be able to flow out of us to others.

Therefore, to have clean sons, for clean sons to be born, it is necessary that a clean word comes forth (where the *Word* is the seed that flows from God) and also a clean people to receive it. If a clean word and clean people exist, then God will be able to multiply them and more spiritual births will take place.

None of us in our own nature can say that we represent God, because we can't. I was explaining to a pastor why it is that I don't want to participate in politics (there is a new Christian political party being created), and I told him that I don't want to participate in politics because I would have to lie. I would have to say that I am very good and because of that goodness, I would want people to vote for me, when in reality I am not that good.

The Lord Jesus said, *Why dost thou call me good? There is none good but one, that is, God,* and the Lord Himself would not have been good if He had not done the will of the Father at all times. Therefore, if I am going to start a political career saying that I am bad, then who is going to vote for me?

But here is the truth. The solution to our problems is not going to come through politics. It is pleasant when politics are clean and adjust themselves to the truth. That is important. But our salvation does not come like that, because we are not looking for the things of this world in order to be saved. For the kingdom of God is not of this world; rather, it is a kingdom that has to start in each of our hearts. The Lord was not looking to be the emperor; He was not looking to be the governor in Jerusalem. He is looking for a totally different kingdom, the kingdom of God.

Going back to Ezra, the Israelite people in Babylon (Babylon is a type and shadow of man involved in confused religious systems) and the vessels of the temple of God ended up in the temple of Babylon (the vessels of the temple of God represent the ministers that God has and that He will use to serve and bless others), and they were locked up. This was a sentence upon the people that the Lord dictated for seventy years because the people of God had been careless. God said through the mouth of the prophet Jeremiah:

> 1 *Run ye to and fro through the streets of Jerusalem and see now and find out and seek in the broad places thereof, if ye can find a man, if there be any that execute judgment, that seek the truth; and I will pardon the city* (Jeremiah 5:1).

If there had been one clean man, God would have set the people free. But this one man could not be found because he did not exist. Outside of God there is none clean; therefore, captivity came upon the people of God.

But in the book of Ezra, we see this people coming out of captivity because the Lord declared that it was time to go back and rebuild the temple of the Lord. And we are in such a day. We are in the time that the Lord has declared to rebuild His temple, not just rebuild it as individuals rebuilt it in Babylon, but now He is going to unite us by the Spirit of God. The first thing we see in the book of Ezra is that to rebuild the temple the people used voluntary gifts, not obligatory tithes. The gifts were voluntary as each one gave freely from their heart.

> 1 *Then rose up the heads of the families of Judah and of Benjamin and the priests and the Levites, of all those whose Spirit God woke up to go up to build the house of the LORD which is in Jerusalem* (Ezra 1:5).

God is waking the Spirit in His people to give them the vision of the clean bride that the Lord wants. This temple cannot be built in Babylon; it cannot even be built in the desert. It must be built in

Jerusalem within the Promised Land, within the inheritance that is promised to the sons of God. At this moment, this inheritance is filled with weeds and rubble; it is filled with those who are managing God's inheritance the wrong way.

When the people of Israel were headed to rebuild the temple of the Lord, a problem came up that had to resolved. All of the priests who could not prove their lineage or what tribe they were from were cast out of the priesthood because they were considered contaminated.

> 59 *And these were those which went up from Telmelah, Telharsa, Cherub, Addan, and Immer, but they could not show their father's house and their seed, whether they were of Israel.*
>
> 60 *The sons of Delaiah, the sons of Tobiah, the sons of Nekoda, six hundred and fifty-two.*
>
> 61 *And of the sons of the priests: the sons of Habaiah, the sons of Koz, the sons of Barzillai; who took a wife of the daughters of Barzillai, the Gileadite, and was called after their name.*
>
> 62. *These sought their register among those that were reckoned by genealogy, but they were not found; therefore, they were, as polluted, put from the priesthood* (Ezra 2:59-62).

We are now in the time in which there is a priesthood in all the people of God; all can have direct communion with God, and all can help others to have communion with God (which is the work of a priest). But there are two seeds: one is corruptible and the other incorruptible. Many people within the people of God have received the corruptible seed; they have received a false gospel and a false spirit. Those who cannot prove that their seed is incorruptible will be cast out of the priesthood because they are contaminated and not worthy of this new thing that the Lord is doing.

In Babylon, it is possible to work in any way you want. In Babylon, there could be pastors preaching one thing and living another. There could be priests preaching one way and living another way. But the temple of God that is within the true inheritance of the people of God (which is something that has to do with heavenly or spiritual realms) can only be built by those with clean hearts; all others will be cast away from the priesthood because they are contaminated.

When the people got to Jerusalem, the first thing they did was to restore the altar.

> 1 *And when the seventh month was come and the sons of Israel were in the cities, the people gathered themselves together as one man in Jerusalem.*
>
> 2 *Then stood up Jeshua, the son of Jozadak, and his brethren the priests, and Zerubbabel, the son of Shealtiel, and his brethren, and they built the altar of the God of Israel, to offer burnt offerings upon it, as it is written in the law of Moses, the man of God.*
>
> *And they set the altar upon its bases, for fear was upon them because of the peoples of those lands, and they offered burnt offerings upon it unto the LORD, even burnt offerings morning and evening* (Ezra 3:1 2).

The altar represents the conditions of the gospel, the conditions in which we come to the Lord. We have to come to the Lord in His way, not any other way that a group may have as a norm. Many people say, "Come, receive the Lord and He will give you everything you want. Receive Christ and He will give you money, a house, a car; anything you want."

But the true gospel is: "Come to Christ and that will be the way of the cross, and the Lord will finish off everything that is not good in you, and you will be born again as a new creature." The Lord will create and fortify the new man, but at the same time He will destroy and kill the old man. This is a gospel that many people do not want to receive, and many others do not want to preach.

After setting the altar the way it was supposed to be, three kinds of sacrifices were made. The first sacrifice represented sin. A calf was brought in, and the priests would lay hands on it (the calf represented sin). They would bleed it on the altar and burn it, symbolizing that God wanted to take the life from sin, so sin would not live in them anymore. It would lose its strength to manage and manipulate their lives. This is why sin is to be burned in God's fire until it is consumed. God's power is not solely to forgive us of our sins, but also to cleanse us of all unrighteousness.

The second sacrifice was the guilt offering. After the Lord delivers us from sin, the enemy comes and wants to put guilt upon us for what we have done. So another animal was taken (symbolizing guilt), and it too was bled and burned on the altar. This is what the Lord wants to do with guilt. He wants to totally finish with guilt so we can be in liberty to do His will.

Then came the third sacrifice which was a peace offering. Perhaps the most important, this peace offering symbolizes a person whose heart is right with God, who is already justified, redeemed, filled with the Holy Spirit, and clean before the Lord; where everything that the Lord is, everything that He has done, already comes as a clean sacrifice, a living sacrifice to be presented ready for God.

It is not for us to grab these gifts, this cleanliness, and this glorious liberty that the Lord has given us, and do whatever we want with it. But it is for us to go back to God and do His will and learn to do it

His way. These are the three sacrifices first described in Leviticus Chapter 7, and this process is called reconciliation. It is the ministry of reconciliation that the Lord has given which is the first thing that was restored in Jerusalem.

After restoring the altar, the next thing to restore was the temple. A new foundation had to be put in place, a new base – the cornerstone. We know who that cornerstone is; it is our Lord Jesus, as the *only* Master and Lord, and everything we do must be committed to His will. He is the cornerstone, the stone that the builders rejected to later build a house that was not the house of God; it was the house of religion.

Now the Lord wants to *show the House to the house,* and that can't be done just with books (though we have a series of books under that name). The only way to fully do it is with a people with clean hearts, a people who are flowing in the Spirit of God, a people who are worshiping before a restored altar, a people who have been set free of sin and guilt and are offering themselves as living, clean sacrifices before the Lord. All of these stones will be built in relation to the cornerstone of the Lordship and dominion of Jesus Christ.

After these things happened, problems continued at the work site. When we want to do God's will God's way, someone is going to come and try to stop the work.

> 4 *Then the people of the land weakened the hands of the people of Judah and troubled them in building*
>
> 5 *and hired counsellors against them, to frustrate their counsel, all the days of Cyrus, king of Persia, even until the reign of Darius, king of Persia* (Ezra 4:4-5).

Not only that, but they also wrote letters to the king.

11 *This is the copy of the letter that they sent: Unto Artaxerxes, the king: Thy servants, the men of the other side of the river, and of Cheenet.*

12 *Be it known unto the king that the Jews who came up from thee to us are come unto Jerusalem, building the rebellious and the bad city, and have founded the walls thereof and joined the foundations.*

13 *Be it known now unto the king, that, if this city is rebuilt, and the walls founded, they will not pay toll, tribute, and custom, and so the revenue of the kings shall be reduced.*

14 *Now because we are salted with the salt of the palace, and it is not just unto us to see the king's dishonour; therefore, we have sent to make this known unto the king,*

15 *that search may be made in the book of the records of our fathers; so shalt thou find in the book of the records and know that this city is a rebellious city and hurtful unto kings and provinces and that from old time they form rebellions in the midst of her, for which cause this city was destroyed.*

16 *We notify the king that if this city is built again, and its walls founded, the portion on the other side of the river shall no longer be yours* (Ezra 4:11-16).

When someone begins to preach God's way, those who have their own kingdoms in churches notice that if the true message of the Lord sets in the hearts of those that listen, their own little kingdoms will no longer be theirs. Therefore, they try to stop the work because those who will listen and begin to be led by the Spirit will no longer obey them.

In Ezra 5, Haggai and Zechariah began to prophesy by saying, "Even though the king says one thing, God says another, and God's order is to continue with the work." When the king's men came and asked who gave them authorization to do this, look at the answer:

> 4 *Then we said unto them regarding this, These are the names of the men that make this building!* (Ezra 5:4, the Spanish translation *Casidoro de Reina* has an exclamation mark and not a question mark).

They began with the names of the apostolic people that God had appointed to make this building. This authorization was more powerful than the king's word, to the point of stopping his messengers who had to go back with this news to the king. When we do things in the nature of God, He gives us a new name. God changes our name for His.

The Lord took all that was ours when He died for us, and when He sends us to do something in His name, we have the authority to do it above anything that may come against it. It does not matter who gives the order to stop. If God gives the order to continue, no one will be able to stop it as long as we have restored the altar, put up the true foundation, and made sure we kept our hearts clean. If we are working in the nature of God and we answer with that name, that is, His name over ours, no one can stop us. This is the lesson in the book of Ezra and in the book of Nehemiah.

So what happened then? The king changed his mind and took the rest of the vessels of gold and silver that were in Babylon and sent them back with a tremendous offering. The king said, "I have to support this work, because why would I want anathema over me and my sons?"

The king himself understood the way that God works, and a fear of God began to take hold of the king of the king. The king himself commanded that all of the expenses be charged to the royal treasury.

At the beginning they were saying, "If you let them continue this work you are not going to have any more tributes or taxes," and the work was stopped. Now God turns everything around, and it is God's children who get the tributes and the taxes of the entire world, and they use them to construct the building. But note that this is after the work has begun in God's way, after He has a free and pure priesthood.

There is another factor here in the book of Ezra. Ezra became discouraged because he saw that the people of God, beginning with the leaders and the priests, had mixed themselves with the women of the land. Even King Solomon in all his wisdom sinned in the same way (with strange women), causing the division of his kingdom.

> 1 *Now when these things were done, the princes came to me, saying, The people of Israel and the priests and the Levites, have not separated themselves from the peoples of the lands of the Canaanites, the Hittites, the Perizzites, the Jebusites, the Ammonites, the Moabites, the Egyptians, and the Amorites, doing according to their abominations,*
>
> 2 *for they have taken of their daughters for themselves and for their sons, and the holy seed is mingled with the peoples of the lands; and the hand of the princes and of the governors has been foremost in this trespass.*
>
> 3 *And when I heard this thing, I rent my garment and my mantle and plucked off of the hair of my head and of my beard and sat down astonied.*
>
> 4 *Then each one that trembled at the words of the God of Israel because of the transgression of those that had been carried away were assembled unto me; and I sat astonied until the evening sacrifice.*
>
> 5 *And at the evening sacrifice I arose up from my affliction; and having rent my garment and my mantle, I fell upon my*

knees and spread out my hands unto the LORD my God
(Ezra 9:1-5).

All of these details are important and we could easily preach on the book of Ezra for a whole week, because all of the names and all of the numbers are significant, and all of it has important information for us.

What follows is that the people of God made a new covenant to cleanse themselves and get rid of those women and all of their sons.

2 Then Shechaniah, the son of Jehiel, one of the sons of Elam, answered and said unto Ezra, We have rebelled against our God and have taken strange women of the peoples of the land, but there is yet hope for Israel concerning this thing.

3 Now, therefore, let us make a covenant with our God to send away all the women and such as are born of them, according to the counsel of the Lord and of those that fear the commandment of our God; and let it be done according to the law (Ezra 10:2-3).

Later in Nehemiah, it says that they had sons that could not speak the language of the Jews; they could not speak the language of God. They could only speak it when mixed with other languages.

23 In those days I also saw Jews that had married wives of Ashdod, of Ammon, and of Moab;

24 and their sons spoke half in the speech of Ashdod, and according to the language of each people; for they could not speak in the Jews' language.

25 And I contended with them and cursed them and smote certain of them and plucked off their hair and made them swear by God, saying, Ye shall not give your daughters unto their sons nor take their daughters unto your sons, or for yourselves.

26 Did not Solomon, king of Israel, sin by these things? Yet among many nations there was no king like him, who was beloved of his God, and God made him king over all Israel; nevertheless, strange women caused even him to offend (Nehemiah 13:23-26).

Today, the same thing occurs in the church. We have many people who cannot speak God's language; they mix the language of God with the language of the world. We are not speaking of men getting rid of their wives or children, or applying this part of the Scripture to their marriages, because this is a spiritual example, since the natural part happened many years ago with Israel. We are speaking of a clean ministry that is sharing the true Word of God. If the Lord is truly flowing through a ministry, the fruit thereof is a clean seed that comes from God. Therefore, there is not yet a minister who can say, "I am the husband; I am the one who is going to give birth to spiritual sons!"

Ezra and Nehemiah are examples of the Holy Spirit of God working through people. Even though the Holy Spirit is invisible, He works through people. We can also see it in Abraham's servant who went to find a wife for Isaac. We can also see it in many of us. But we can't say that any of these men, or us, *are* the Holy Spirit.

So if the Holy Spirit is flowing through a person who has a clean heart, then the pure seed (masculine gender as in *sons*) is also flowing. But to be able to produce clean sons of God, it is necessary to have a clean woman, a clean bride. Because as a group we are always referred to in the Scriptures in feminine form, we are that woman the Lord wants to bring to Himself to marry with the purpose being to multiply clean sons of God.

When the people who are supposed to be flowing in the Spirit and giving a true word are not careful with what kind of *women* (or congregation) they mingle with, the result is an impure seed. This is happening today with pastors who know what a true and clean gospel is, but do not teach it to the people for fear of losing some of them or upsetting some of them.

Even though these pastors know what the narrow gate is, they preach a wider gate because they don't want to lose the offerings or the people. Therefore, a mixing of seed occurs. We find people with a corruptible seed in them, and because of this, they desire worldly things. We find some other people trying to plant a spiritual word in those hearts, and we see it doesn't work. To rebuild the temple of God, there must be a clean word, and it must be received by a clean people to produce clean spiritual sons.

Many people believe that the pastors (or shepherds) are the ones who are supposed to produce sheep, but this is impossible. The sheep are the ones who are supposed to produce more sheep; and it is the sheep who should help raise the newborn sheep. This is the way that God's people are going to multiply.

But even when there is a clean word, if it is received by a congregation that is not clean, bastard sons are born who cannot receive the inheritance of God. The result is that after a certain time, the Lord leaves, and man continues with his religion, and the multiplication of the sons is done man's way.

The children of Israel came to this point:

> 1 *And it came to pass in the month Nisan, in the twentieth year of Artaxerxes, the king, that as wine was before him, I took up the wine and gave it unto the king. And as I had not been sad before in his presence,*

2 the king said unto me, Why is thy countenance sad, seeing thou art not sick? This is nothing else but brokenness of heart. Then I was very sore afraid

3 and said unto the king, Let the king live for ever; why should not my countenance be sad, when the city, the house of my fathers' sepulchres, lies waste, and its gates are consumed with fire?

4 Then the king said unto me, For what dost thou make request? So I prayed to the God of the heavens.

5 And I said unto the king, If it pleases the king, and if thy servant has found favour in thy sight, that thou would send me unto Judah, unto the city of my fathers' sepulchres, that I may rebuild it.

6 Then the king said unto me (the queen also sitting by him), For how long shall thy journey be, and when wilt thou return? So the matter pleased the king, and he sent me; and I set him a time (Nehemiah 2:1-6).

Nehemiah was the one who brought the cup to the king, the one who gave him the wine. The wine is a type and shadow of new life and joy. The meaning of the walls of the city is very important to us because God's people today have no protection; even those who are going back to Jerusalem are exposed to tremendous dangers. When the walls of the city are built, two things happen: first, there is protection; and second, there is a separation where it is well known who is inside and who is outside.

The people who have a clean seed and look for purity and holiness are inside, and the rest are left outside. The people who love to live the way they want to live don't like it when the wall is built, when things are defined. In Nehemiah, when the people of Israel began to rebuild the wall, the first gate that was restored was the gate of the sheep, and the second gate was the gate of the fish. When the Lord defines how life is in the kingdom of God and how life is outside the kingdom of God, the first thing that He defines is the entry for the sheep and then the entry for the fish. The fish symbolizes those who are in the world, but are waiting to be fished for the kingdom of God.

After the gates came the tower of the furnaces, and many things symbolize this process: the dealings of God. When the Lord begins to apply not only the fire of His love, but also the fire of His justice to everything, the result is that you come into His life or you completely go out of His path, which implies a full separation.

At the end of the restoration, Nehemiah established the gatekeepers. He also prohibited men from carrying their own burdens on God's day. He established singers, and the people of Israel began to celebrate the Feast of Tabernacles. They sounded the trumpet and read the law; they began to see that they were doing things God's way.

In the end, God's glory was *almost* restored in Israel. Everything ended up providing many examples for us, but God's glory never came. Through the passing of time, Israel continued with many tragedies, to the point that there was not a prophet in Israel for four hundred years until the time of our Lord Jesus.

I discovered something here that I believe explains why we have not come into the fullness of the glory of God in the restoration that was presented to the people of Israel. In Nehemiah 6:15, they finished the wall. In Nehemiah 7, they set the doors down and established doorkeepers, singers, and Levites. In Nehemiah 8, the whole town joined as one man in the plaza that is in front of the water gate (they were ready to receive the water of life). Then, in Nehemiah 9 it says:

14 *and didst make known unto them the sabbath of thy holiness and didst prescribe for them commandments, statutes, and law by the hand of Moses, thy servant* (Nehemiah 9:14).

The Lord made them to know the Sabbath of His holiness, the rest, the true rest of the Lord. Besides this, they passed through the restoration of the song of the Lord; they entered into the Feast of Trumpets to receive the message God's way. The first thing that this produced was a tremendous sorrow and repentance, and then a tremendous joy and jubilee. But they committed an error:

29 *Strengthened with their brethren, their nobles* [this word refers to those that were born free, who are not slaves; and there were already babies being born in the land where there was slavery, but look what they did], *they came forward in an oath with a curse that they would walk in God's law, which was given by the hand of Moses, the servant of God, and observe and do all the commandments of the LORD our Lord, and his judgments and his statutes;*

30 *and that we would not give our daughters unto the peoples of the land nor take their daughters for our sons* (Nehemiah 10:29-30).

Collectively they made an oath that if they did not fulfill the law of God, a curse would fall upon them. This was the error. This is where they failed because no one is able to fulfill God's law in their own strength. When they made this oath with a curse, they then secured the curse upon themselves, because sooner or later they were going to fail, and the curse was going to fall upon them. This is the problem with the Old Covenant.

God's law is good, but no one can keep it by his own strength. It wasn't until the coming of our Lord Jesus, until the New Covenant, the law written in our hearts, the law by grace with the power of God in us that we are able to enter into a covenant to keep the law of God. This is a covenant of blessing.

The Lord says that we were taught by an oath, but now He is telling us not to swear by heaven or by Jerusalem or by anything else, but let our yea be yea and our nay be nay. He says that anything more than that comes from the evil one and this evil one has brought curses over God's people.

Religion has always tried to bring people under an oath of curse. The pastor will say, "Who is going to be committed to come every Sunday at nine?" Then the entire church swears by it and takes an oath, and sure enough one person is not able to go on that day and at that hour and a curse comes upon that person.

"Who is going to be committed to give tithes?" The people get motivated, and many say that they will until the day comes when they will not be able to bring tithes. Because of the oath that they took, a curse comes upon them. They are manipulated by guilt trips and finally sin revives, guilt revives, and all the process of reconciliation with the Lord gets undone, leaving only a people of God who, when you look at their lives, show no difference between them and the world. We see the same number of divorces, robberies, and all kinds of illicit activities in the people of God as are in the world.

Not long ago in the United States, the statistics of Christians and non-Christians were equal: an equal number of abortions, an equal number of divorces, an equal number of drug-addicted children, etc. All were equal; there was no radical change that should have distinguished all of God's people. The people who enter the blessing of God must remain marked, being totally different from the world; although we live in the world, we are not to be of the world.

Then here is the error, and it is the error that continues to be committed, the same error in the book of Ezra of contaminating the seed of God with the *women* who were not clean. This is literally happening in the people of God, because many men are not faithful to their wives and continue to be contaminated with strange women. But the worst damage is that which is happening spiritually in the church, where we are *not* seeking a clean word to come out and be sown in a clean people.

At the end of the book of Nehemiah, look at what happened:

And the priests and the Levites purified themselves and puri-
fied the people and the gates and the wall (Nehemiah 12:30).

Everything was cleaned; that is what the Lord wants. That cleansing served for that generation, and that generation had the blessing of God; but that generation lost it later by the oath of a curse.

To give this sketch in another way, in Zechariah 6, we read the story of a people coming out of Babylon on their way to Jerusalem to rebuild the temple (God's kingdom). They had to pass between two brass mountains in the desert. Those two bronze mountains symbolize the judgments of God to remove everything that is not good in us.

Zechariah 6 and 7 are parallel with Revelation 6 and 7. In comparing these chapters, we can see the difference between the ways of the Old Covenant versus the ways of the New Covenant, where the New Covenant is a lot better. In Zechariah 6, there are four colors of horses; and in Revelation 6, there also are four colors of horses, but with some important differences.

To give a global example and to conclude this word, the following shows the difference between the chapters:

1 And I turned and lifted up my eyes and looked, and, behold, there came four chariots out from between two mountains, and those mountains were of brass.

2 In the first chariot were red horses and in the second chariot black horses;

3 in the third chariot white horses and in the fourth chariot grisled and bay horses.

4 Then I answered and said unto the angel that talked with me, What is this, my lord?

5 And the angel answered and said unto me, These are the four spirits of the heavens, which go forth from standing before the Lord of all the earth (Zechariah 6:1-6).

In this passage we see that in the first chariot there were red horses, in the second chariot black horses, in the third one white horses, and in the fourth one grisled and bay horses. Furthermore, Zechariah explains that these are the four spirits of God that go throughout the earth. The horses symbolize the work of the Holy Spirit in us. In the Old Testament, the Spirit of God was in the prophets, but did not enter all the people at the same time. In the New Testament, the Holy Spirit can be in everyone at the same time, this is the great difference. It is the difference of redemption that the Lord accomplished for us.

1 And I saw when the Lamb had opened the first seal, and I heard the first of the four animals, saying as with a voice of thunder, Come and see.

2 And I saw and, behold, a white horse; and he that was seated upon him had a bow, and a crown was given unto him, and he went forth victorious, that he might also overcome.

3 And when he had opened the second seal, I heard the second animal, which said, Come and see.

4 And another horse went forth that was red, and unto him that was seated thereon was given power to take away the peace of the earth and that they should kill one another; and there was given unto him a great sword.

5 And when he had opened the third seal, I heard the third animal, which said, Come and see. And I saw and, behold, a black horse, and he that was seated upon him had a yoke in his hand.

6 And I heard a voice in the midst of the four animals, which said, A choenix of wheat for a denarius and three choenix of barley for a denarius; and see thou hurt not the oil and the wine.

7 And when he had opened the fourth seal, I heard the voice of the fourth animal, which said, Come and see.

8 And I looked and, behold, a green horse, and he that was seated upon him was named Death, and Hades followed with him. And power was given unto him over the fourth part of the earth, to kill with sword and with hunger and with death and with the beasts of the earth (Revelation 6:1-8).

Now in Zechariah 6 the first horse was red; in Revelation the first horse is white. Before the sacrifice of Christ, the people had to offer sacrifices of blood every day for all the crimes and sins they had committed. The maximum they could achieve was to be clean and in peace for a year on the Day of Atonement, because the next year they had to do it all over again.

However, the sacrifice that Christ made is forever (we will explain it later). In Revelation 6, we come at once to a white horse – the one that comes into this New Covenant with God, God's way, and the one that comes to the restored altar of God. This one lets God kill the sin and the guilt that continues His life as a living sacrifice to God and enters in cleanliness. We cannot achieve cleanliness and holiness with experience after twenty or thirty years. Cleanliness and holiness comes when God declares it, but we must be careful to walk in holiness with Him, because we can lose it if we stain our garments with sin.

The difference between the Old Covenant and the New Covenant is that in the New Covenant we enter in with the white horse. In the Old Covenant, the people had to pass first through the red horse, then the black horse, and finally the white horse.

In Revelation 6, in the New Covenant, we immediately enter into holiness as soon as the Lord saves us, and it is not just future salvation. It is also an immediate salvation from the power of sin. The Lord Jesus is at the right hand of the Father as the mediator of the covenant. He, through the Holy Spirit of God, applies the blood.

Regarding the second horse (the red horse), we read that a great sword is given to him, and it is the Lord that has that sword because He is the one that applies the blood, and He does so using the sword. People walk around saying that they are *under the Blood* thinking that it is a magic formula. To say "Blood of Christ cover me" is to ask the Lord to bring the sword down on us and to separate between soul and spirit, between that which is from God and that which isn't. To say this is to ask Him to cut off all that is not good and to circumcise our heart.

Now comes the black horse. The black horse is the way of the Lord that to our carnal eye seems black. It does not appeal to us to pick up His cross and follow Him, because at the end it will lead us to crucifixion, and that crucifixion will be ours, and that is a path too dark to take. We can only walk this path when the Holy Spirit is within us guiding us, and not only guiding us, but also empowering us.

This is the reason the people in the Old Testament failed; they had to start with the red horse and continue with the black horse. This path is difficult to follow because through the law (our own strength) no one can attain the white horse of holiness. Only the one that was able to go through the red and the black horses was able to reach that holiness.

But in the New Covenant, the white horse, the horse that symbolizes holiness, goes in first, entering at once into the glorious victory of the sons of God. To maintain that victory, He applies the blood and lowers the sword wherever and whenever necessary. He is the one that makes us walk in a path that to the natural eye seems dark and difficult, but He is taking us to life, to victory, and to the blessing.

> And when he had opened the third seal, I heard the third
> animal, which said, Come and see. And I saw and, behold,
> a black horse, and he that was seated upon him had a yoke
> in his hand (Revelation 6:5).

One word here was translated wrong. In the original, it doesn't say *a pair of balances in his hand*; it says *a yoke in his hand*. The translators didn't know how to translate this portion because the literal translation doesn't seem to fit here. The black horse symbolizes God's yoke. To take God's yoke upon us seems like a dark path to take, for it means the way of the cross; however, it is also a very easy path to take because we know that his yoke is easy and his burden is light. The Lord is also in this yoke with us providing all of the strength needed.

The passage goes on in verse 6 to say, *A choenix of wheat for a denarius.* A yoke was necessary to have on an ox to till the ground and be able to produce wheat. A *denarius* meant a day's wages. A day walking with God and the reward is a measure of wheat, or bread, our spiritual food that we need for that day (our daily bread). This is the first feast, the Passover, the feast of entering into that direct dealing with God.

Verse 6 continues: *and three choenix of barley for a denarius.* If we continue with the Lord, He begins to bless us, and we enter into the Feast of Pentecost. We receive from him the gifts of the Holy Spirit of God, and He gives us even more blessing than we need. We must decide what we should do with our blessing. Are we going to use it for ourselves and build our own kingdoms or are we going to use it to flow in His Spirit, using these gifts that the Lord has given us to bless others? The same day's work and in exchange three measures means that if we continue walking with God in Pentecost, He will bless us above and beyond our own needs so that we can be a blessing to others.

Then comes the third feast, the Feast of Tabernacles, but it comes with a change. God doesn't say *ten measures of wine and oil;* He doesn't say *twenty measures* or *a hundred measures.* He doesn't give a number, because this last feast is unlimited. But there is a little problem here. He says, *and see thou hurt not the oil and the wine,* because the person that is not faithful with the little, even that little which he has will be taken from him.

So what does this mean? It means that the person who is not faithful with the gifts in the Feast of Pentecost is not going to receive the unlimited wine of the new life, nor the oil of the unlimited anointing in the Feast of Tabernacles. We can compare this with the people in Ezra and Nehemiah when they were celebrating the Feast of Tabernacles. For the first time in Israel, they lived in booths. The Bible says they had never lived in booths before.

The Lord is bringing His people to the knowledge that we must leave the house or habitation that we have always known and come and live a different way and do things God's way. This booth is a type and shadow of what Christ did when He left His glory and came to dwell in a different tabernacle, a human body like ours.

So we go through all of these dealings of God that now are much easier because we have the strength of the Holy Spirit inside us, and now we come to the last horse. In Zechariah 6, the fourth horse was grisled and bay. This last horse symbolizes death; it is a horse that is described as something totally disgusting. Death is something that used to grab people and would not let them go; even Abraham and the patriarchs were prisoners in Sheol before the sacrifice of Christ.

The Bible says that when the Lord descended to Sheol, He took captivity captive; He took those who belonged to Him and broke the jail that the devil had. This is the reason the fourth horse in Revelation 6 is so different. Verse 8 says: *And I looked and, behold, a green horse* [the word here is not *pale*; the literal translation is *green*; the translation uses the word *pale* but in every other place of the Bible, this word is translated *green*]. This green horse is something that doesn't occur in nature as we know it, because the purpose of God is to take us out of that nature in order for us to be a new creation.

Green horses don't exist, but in His nature, God creates this green horse symbolic of resurrection life. The Scripture continues: *and he that was seated upon him was named Death, and Hades followed with him. And power was given unto him over the fourth part of the earth, to kill with sword and with hunger and with death and with the beasts of the earth.* Death has always been an enemy of the people of God; those who have wanted to walk God's way have been killed.

In the early church there was a saying: *the blood of the martyrs is the seed of the church.* But with Christ's death, there was victory over death because now, to be absent from this body is to be present with the Lord. So now, death loses its strength and those who die in Christ have hope, which is portrayed by the green horse. Green is the color of resurrection and life. Death is now a path to eternal life, and that is why we have the color green instead of a dirty, grisled and bay color.

So instead of a grisled and bay horse of Zechariah or a mistranslated pale horse, we have the green horse of righteousness and hope, the green horse of that new resurrection life in Christ. He takes death and gets rid of our old life, destroying it as He does with everything that is not good in us. The grave error in many churches is that they are trying to rehabilitate the old man when God is trying to kill him. They are trying to organize something that God wants to get rid of. God wants the old to pass away, and all things to be made new.

If we continue in Zechariah, we come to the point when the priesthood is already clean and we see crowns, dominion, glory, and blessings. The only problem is that the people could not go through the stage of the chariots because they were never able to go through the stage of the black horse. They didn't have the strength of the Spirit of God to take them through God's paths.

Instead, the path that we see in Revelation gives us the opportunity to do so, but the modern church took this path and changed it. It took the path that we read of in Revelation 6 and said this is a big calamity and curse that will come upon the earth. It continued doing things the way they were being done in Zechariah 6. The church today continues making promises to God and oaths under the curse. Therefore, the church still is under curse and has never been able to come out into blessing because they have never let the Spirit of God have His freedom.

We know that the Lord is going to return, and when the fifth seal is opened, it tells us exactly when it is that He is coming.

> 9 *And when he had opened the fifth seal, I saw under the altar*
> *the souls of those that had been slain because of the word of*
> *God and for the testimony which they held* (Revelation 6:9).

This is a process that can happen right now in our own lives while we are still here on this earth. For God is trying to do the work of killing off the old nature while giving us His new nature. This is also applied to those who are literally dead with the Lord and are under the altar in the heavens; it is applied in two ways:

> 10 *And they cried with a loud voice, saying, How long, O Lord,*
> *holy and true, dost thou not judge and avenge our blood on*
> *those that dwell in the earth?* (Revelation 6:10).

The earth is the symbol of the church, and the church has persecuted the real Christians throughout history. The pagan Rome killed a few million, the Inquisition made by the church killed more than seventy million, and we continue with the Inquisition as we verbally kill the reputation of those who do not fit with our own system.

> 11 *And white robes were given unto each one of them*
> (Revelation 6:11).

This means that individually they were given robes; we are to answer to God for ourselves. Each one of us has to come individually into holiness unto the Lord, first covered by the holiness of Christ, but secondly walking with Him until this holiness becomes real in us. Many believe that Christ paid a sum when He really gave His life as a ransom for many to purchase us. If He had paid a sum for us like paying a debt in the bank, we would be saved whether we accept it or not. If you have a debt in a bank and someone pays it for you, the debt is paid whether you know it or not.

But this is not the case with Christ. The Lord Jesus did not pay a debt. What he did was to die and shed His blood. What he did was to die in the flesh so we can have the opportunity to be a part of Him. If we are identified in that death, it means that we are not going to live for ourselves anymore, but that we are going to be governed and led by Him (we are not our own).

His death covers us; but how does it cover us? Well, in the same way that an investigation cannot be opened against a dead man. Here in Colombia, there was a process to try to confiscate the properties and real estate of some big drug lords. The problem was that some of them had been dead for some time. When the government went to take the properties from Gonzalo Rodríguez Gacha (a very famous and one of the biggest drug lords in Colombia), he had been dead for some time, and they couldn't do it because when he died, all legal processes were canceled. Legally you can't process a dead man.

So if we are dead in Christ, all legal processes against us are cancelled, and this is the way that Christ saves us. It is not that He suffered a little bit more on the cross because I lied, and a little bit more if I stole a million dollars, or that He suffered a little bit for each sin of every person. No. He died one time and for all and now gives us the opportunity to be a part of this many-membered body of Christ. The condition to be part of this many-membered body is that we are to not insist on our own will, but to surrender to His will and accept His government over us. This is salvation, very simply.

But man has taken it and made it very difficult. From this misunderstanding came the idea of purgatory, and in evangelical circles we have doctrines of irresistible grace or *once saved always saved*, with no emphasis on how we live our lives, and many other lies are openly taught. Why? Because man does not want to surrender his own will. Man wants a system of salvation that will allow him to continue imposing his own will, which is impossible.

11 *And it was said unto them, that they should rest yet for a little while until their fellow servants and their brethren, that should be killed as they were, should be fulfilled* (Revelation 6:11).

Here we know when it is that the Lord will be returning: when the number of those He has in mind is complete, when the number of those that will be saved is complete, when the many-membered body that He has in mind has the number of members that He has purposed in His heart from the beginning. When all of this is complete, then He will come.

The Lord knows how many He needs to put a just government on earth. He knows how many He needs to delegate authority and responsibility over the entire universe. He has a purpose in His heart, and He is not going to close the door before it comes to pass. Only He knows how many. When the last one chosen is sealed, when the last one chosen enters into the plan of redemption, then He will close the curtain, and He will return and it will be the Day of Judgment.

Look what happens after this when the sixth seal is opened:

12 *And I saw when he had opened the sixth seal, and, behold, there was a great earthquake.*

An earthquake is when the earth is shaken, or, as in this passage, when the church, symbolized by the earth and related to the Promised Land, is shaken. God wants a clean people, and to obtain this, He will shake the church in such a way that everything that is not His will has to come out.

And the sun became black as sackcloth of hair.

The sun is the symbol of this world, and there is nothing new under the sun, said Solomon. There is nothing new, but we are looking for a new sun. We are looking for the Sun of Righteousness where there is a new creation, and we can be part of this new creation because it is a work that He does in us, straight from our hearts. So the sun of this world will become black; it will get dark, and we are seeing it now.

People are living in this world under corruption, mafias, etc. These people are now in a bit of a problem because their time is getting dark, their sun is setting, and one day it will set forever. It will not just be for a period of time; it will be forever. But some other people are seeing that the Lord is using this quake. They are seeing a new sun rising; it is becoming easier to share and explain the gospel. Others are seeing that the Word of God is flowing out in a better and cleaner way than ever before. They are seeing lives being transformed for real, and all of this that we see in the midst of confusion gives us joy because we see that He has not forsaken us nor left us.

And the moon became as blood (Revelation 6:12).

The moon is the symbol of the church. There have been many wars in the church (many of them in Europe), and many of them were because of the Catholic Church, but the evangelical churches don't come out of this clean either because the evangelical church has also made terrible wars. Maybe not so much in the way of killing one another, but they have killed each other with their doctrinal issues, false accusations, and in many other ways. God's people are responsible for many terrible things and also shedding of blood between brothers.

For the people who already see things the way God does, who see all this blood and the sun of this world getting darker, but who already have the work of the Holy Spirit within them and have entered into the death of the old man, the things of this world are no longer an attraction, nor are the churches that practice according to the ways of man. They see the sun as black sackcloth and the moon as blood.

13 *And the stars of heaven fell upon the earth, even as a*
fig tree casts her figs, when she is shaken of a mighty wind
(Revelation 6:13).

The person who doesn't have these direct dealings of God described in the four horses will see some minister who happens to be a good orator and begin to idolize that man. Many other media work the same way, like television for example. It isn't that television is bad in and of itself, but television helps to idolize men. I believe television is a media that can be used correctly when someone with a clean heart is on it.

People who have had the dealings of God in their hearts and have passed through the process of God will see a minister, a good orator with a mighty anointing, but will not idolize the man. They will see the Lord in the man instead of the man himself.

14 *And the heaven departed as a scroll when it is rolled*
together (Revelation 6:14).

The heavens departed. They were opened. When this happens, the people who have the corruptible seed and want to achieve the things of this world, using God's things to manipulate and control other people, begin to look for ways to hide and to cover themselves because they cannot stand God's presence.

The last time that the heavens were opened like a scroll was when Jesus was baptized in the Jordan River. The heavens opened, and the Spirit of God, without measure, descended upon Him. Now the heavens are going to be opened again for a people who are clean, for the people of God who are going through the direct dealings of the Holy Spirit to receive the fullness of the blessing.

We are going to have an open heaven again; this means answered prayers. Our Lord Jesus did not pray prayers that were never answered.

But at the same time He said that He was always doing the will of the Father. Why? Because the heart of the Father and of the Son were in tune; because whatever Jesus was feeling in His heart, the Father was also feeling in His heart. Jesus was able to say, *He that has seen me has seen the Father* He was able to say this because the Father was working through Him.

Now the Lord Jesus is going to have a clean people, a bride right here, and He is going to be able to work through her. It is going to be possible to say, *If you have seen her, you have seen Him.* He is going to be working through her, and when she asks for something, she will be in His will, and He will do it because He loves her and supports her.

> *And the Spirit and the bride say, Come. And let him that hears say, Come. And let him that is thirsty come; and whosoever will, let him take of the water of life freely* (Revelation 22:7).

These two testimonies are the same, instead of a church saying one thing, and the Lord saying another, which is what we have had so far. Judgment is going to come upon all of those who continue to represent God in a wrong way.

> 14 *And every mountain and island were moved out of their places,* [because the only mountain that will stand is His Mountain].

> 15 *And the kings of the earth* [including the kings of the church] *and the princes and the rich and the captains and the strong and every servant and every free man hid themselves in the caves and among the rocks of the mountains*

> 16 *and said to the mountains and to the rocks, Fall on us and hide us from the face of him that is seated upon the throne and from the wrath of the Lamb;*

17 *for the great day of his wrath is come, and who shall be able to stand before him?* (Revelation 6:14-17).

They are not going to be able to stand before the Lord, but there is going to be a people who are going to receive the kingdom, a clean people.

Let us go back to this: they are going to open the seventh seal, and there is silence in the heavens for half an hour. Why is there a silence for half an hour? For two reasons: first, because the true people of God who go before Him do not want to contribute their own ideas any more; they have already learned to be quiet before Him and to listen to Him.

Second, since there is a clean people, the devil, the accuser, who is accusing the brethren day and night, has nothing more to say; he cannot present anymore false accusations before the Lord. So the Lord casts him out of heaven, and there is silence. And the sound of the trumpets of the Word of the Lord in the final hours begin to sound.

In summary, the message of the trumpets and its consequences, which are the vials, is: with the first sound of the trumpet, all the green grass dries up. There are three levels of the Word: first the leaves, then the flower, and then the fruit (Mark 4:28). The Word of God is like the mature grain because it is grain that can be planted and produces more grain. The Lord Jesus was that mature grain that fell into the earth and died to produce more of the same.

In Genesis 1, the grass is given to the beasts for food, but before the fall, the grain is given to the man. The people of God insist on eating grass like beasts do, as Nebuchadnezzar did when he lost his reason and had to eat grass like a beast for a time. Such is the human race, which has lost all reasoning and is eating grass like oxen. People are feeding on something that God created for beasts, but they are not eating the real nurturing food that is for men, the true men, the new man, the new nature.

In the day of the Lord, the possibility to use the things of the Lord to accomplish the things of this world is going to be over. The time for those who are eating the things of God like fat beasts eating grass in the field is going to end. The first trumpet is going to sound, and the message is going to be God's way. Then all that grass is going to dry up, and a tremendous famine will occur, a hunger like the prophet Amos described, a famine for hearing the words of the Lord.

They are going to find out that what they had been eating does not give life. What is going to happen is very interesting. The Lord is going to have a clean people. He is going to have a clean crop. He is going to have a new harvest, and the new thing that He is doing is going to happen at the same time that the old thing is dying.

At this moment, there are many effects, many conditions. Works have been done in the name of God that cannot endure this day and in one way or another will crumble. But the true work that the Lord is doing, the true work that is being planted in the hearts of His people, the pure and clean word that is being planted in a pure people is going to produce clean and pure sons. This is the Feast of Tabernacles.

In the book of Esther there is a feast that symbolizes the wine, the new life in the kingdom. Do you remember that there was a queen who did not want to come at the king's command (Queen *Vashti*, meaning *beautiful*), and she was cast out, and Queen Esther was chosen in her place? She was not only chosen, but she was willing to risk her own life for the lives of her people. And this feast of life that the Lord is inaugurating now is the feast of a people who do not love their own lives.

This way is the victory in Revelation. He will ride the white horse with the sword of truth, with the sign on His thigh, *faithful and truth,* and will be followed by the hosts of heaven that won the victory, *by the blood of the lamb; and the word of their testimony; and they loved not their lives unto the death.* The Lord is bringing this about, and it is going to happen in conditions totally different from the ones we have seen in the church until today. The true battles are not going to happen in the meetings; they are going to happen in daily life, in the daily walk, in the measure that we let the Holy Spirit work in and through us because He is the one who can do it.

The beginning of Revelation 6 says that the one on the white horse went out conquering and to conquer and a bow was given to Him. The Holy Spirit is the one on that white horse with His bow, with His arrows of truth, and it is up to us if we let ourselves be hit by the truth or not. But if He shoots us with His truth, if His truth penetrates deep inside our hearts, everything is going to change in us. He that loves the truth loves the Lord. I know many people who love the truth, but if you were to ask them if they love the Lord, maybe they are not going to be able to answer you because they do not know Him very well. But the person who loves the truth is a prime candidate for this walk because the Lord is the Truth, the Way, and the Life.

Let's pray:

> Father God, we give you thanks for this opportunity that you give us, and we ask you, Lord, that this your Word will penetrate our hearts like an arrow, and that your sword will fall on us to divide soul and spirit, to divide what we are and what you are. I ask you, Lord, for there to be a total transformation in our beings, and not only as individuals, but that there will be a flow of your true body, of this clean bride that you are looking for, and that all of this will be

seen by others. We ask you, Lord, that this be a reality in us, not with an oath under curse, but only by saying yes to your Spirit, saying yes to every change, until everything that does not work in us is changed into the new creation, and that the new man in Christ may be blessed and may go forward in each and every one of us. We ask all of this in the name of our Lord Jesus Christ. Amen.

The Temple – Russell M. Stendal
Original title: El Templo
Translated into English by Cesar and Shannon Trigos
May be freely duplicated as long as the content is not altered

About the Author

Russell Stendal was born in Minneapolis and raised on the mission field in Colombia, South America. He became a missionary jungle pilot at age nineteen. Almost ten years later in 1983, he was kidnapped by Marxist rebels and held hostage for five months. His book, *Rescue the Captors*, relates his experience, including how God worked in the hearts of the rebels.

Russell has written many other books, produced videos, and edited two Bible translations, the Spanish Reina-Valera 2000 and the Jubilee Bible in English.

Russell heads up the work of Colombia Para Cristo, which operates twelve radio stations involving more than one hundred staff and coworkers and covering much of Latin America with the Gospel. A thriving underground church has developed in remote jungle areas of Colombia. New high-gain antennas are now beaming the gospel message deep into areas of increasing crisis across the borders of Venezuela, Ecuador, Peru, and Brazil, as well as throughout Colombia.

Russell and his son Dylan recently wrote a letter to their school concerning issues needing to be addressed. This letter will help any Christian parents or teachers in the United States as well. You can read the letter at: www.scribd.com/doc/146065211/Letter-to-School-Russell-Stendal

www.lamontana.us

Watch the La Montana trailer, a film based on a true Stendal event

Connect with Russell

Email: kiu900@me.com

This book is available from www.lifesentencepublishing.com and amazon.com

Tell others about this book on Facebook

To order more books:

www.lifesentencepublishing.com/Stendal Books

715-223-3013

info@lifesentencepublishing.com